ADRIAN
WALLER'S
GUIDE
TO
MUSIC

1975

LITTLEFIELD, ADAMS & CO.   Totowa, New Jersey

Adrian Waller's guide to Music

First published in the United States 1975 by

LITTLEFIELD, ADAMS & CO.

by special arrangement with Clarke, Irwin & Co., Ltd.

© 1973 by Clarke, Irwin & Company Limited

Printed in Canada

Library of Congress Cataloging in Publication Data

Waller, Adrian
    Adrian Waller's Guide to Music

    (A Littlefield, Adams Quality Paperback No. 296)
    Includes index.
    1. Music—Analysis, appreciation.
    2. Music—History and criticism.   I. Title.
MT6.W1675A3 1975   780'.15   75-2081
ISBN 0-8226-0296-2

For Marie-Claire

ACKNOWLEDGEMENTS

I am indebted to Dr. Floyd Chalmers of Toronto, who read my manuscript and suggested several improvements, and who has been kind enough to contribute a Preface.

I would also like to thank the following organizations and individuals who provided photographs and gave valuable assistance in research:

Angel Records, New York
Ed Archambault Inc., Montreal
Austrian Embassy, Ottawa
Boston Symphony Orchestra, Press Dept.
Mlle Marie Bourbeau, The Montreal Symphony Orchestra
Canadian Broadcasting Corporation
Columbia Records, Toronto
Deutsche Grammophon, Hamburg
D'Oyly Carte Company
Heintzman & Co. Ltd., Toronto
Institute of Italian Culture, Montreal
Gary Jacobs, The Toronto Symphony
Opera Canada
Thad Trottier, RCA Company, Montreal
RCA Company, New York
Stadtverkehrsbüro, Salzburg
Steinway & Sons, New York

I am grateful also to Dianne Vanier and Gillian Moore, who assisted with the typing.

PHOTO CREDITS

Bach—CBC

Handel—Austrian Embassy, Ottawa

Mozart's statue—Stadtverkehrsbüro, Salzburg

Haydn—Austrian Embassy, Ottawa

Beethoven—Austrian Embassy, Ottawa

Beethoven's birthplace—German National Tourist Office, Montreal

Beethoven's bust—Austrian Embassy, Ottawa

Wagner—Austrian Embassy, Ottawa

von Weber—Austrian Embassy, Ottawa

Berlin Chamber Octet—Deutsche Grammophon

Changing of the Guard—Miller Services

Leinsdorf—CBC (Photo, André Le Coz)

Toscanini—RCA

Ormandy and Serkin—RCA

von Karajan—CBC

Bernstein—CBC

Toscanini—RCA

Ozawa—CBC

Barbirolli—Angel

Monteux—RCA

Reiner—RCA

Menuhin—CBC

Koussevitzky—RCA

Beecham—Angel

Mahler—Austrian Embassy, Ottawa

Chopin—*The Gazette,* Montreal

Rubinstein—RCA

Liszt—Austrian Embassy, Ottawa

Alceste—Bibliothèque Nationale, Paris

Cosi Fan Tutte—Opera Canada (Photo, Flaherty)

Aida—Opera Canada

Louis Riel—Photo by Alex Gray

Gershwin—RCA

Brubeck—Columbia

Armstrong—RCA

Ellington—RCA

Goodman—RCA

Junkarov Night Club—Miller Services (Photo, Devaney)

Schubert—Austrian Embassy, Ottawa

Wolf—Austrian Embassy, Ottawa

Strauss, Sr. & Jr.—Austrian Embassy, Ottawa

von Suppé—Austrian Embassy, Ottawa

Ruddigore—The D'Oyly Carte Company

Pinafore—The D'Oyly Carte Company

Lehar, Tauber, Dorsch—Austrian Embassy, Ottawa

Anderson–RCA
Galli-Curci–RCA
Bjoerling–RCA
Phonograph–RCA
Caruso–RCA
Recording session (Ormandy)–RCA
Recording session (informal)–RCA
Barbeau–National Film Board

CONTENTS

PREFACE

One should not begin a preface with a cliché but a cliché happens to identify this book with some precision. "It fills a long felt want."

Mr. Waller tells us, with a happy mixture of captivating fact, pleasing charm and abundant good humour all the things that the lover of music wants to know: what music is; who has given us the music we enjoy; how the great composers—classical and modern—worked; what are the instruments on which it is played, including the human voice.

In between, we are introduced to the Renaissance, the Elizabethan period and the Viennese period; to the great oratorios, operas and operettas. We are told about the piano (and its predecessors the virginal, the spinet and the harpsichord), about the violin and other stringed and reed instruments. We are able to compare the baroque and the romantic composers and the more modern twelve-tone composers and those who have written for electronic music. (I note that Mr. Waller has resisted the temptation to speak of the oboe as "an ill wood-wind that nobody blows good".)

One of the interesting facts that emerge is the considerable number of composers who continued to compose long after they became partially or totally deaf, of whom Beethoven was only one example.

Music, we find, reflects both the temper of its times and the technological advances in the field of mechanics. Science and engineering have both contributed to what we hear. Slavery in the Deep South and the stock market crash of 1929 left their deep impress on composers and performers.

One is surprised to learn that recording of music for replaying has a history that dates back more than a century although the work of Edison and Berliner, in making the phonograph and the durable recording available to millions of music lovers, dates back not much more than 75 years. Greatest of the early recording artists was Enrico Caruso, the most famous tenor of all time, whose records totalled over 200. (But John McCormack was not far behind.)

Mr. Waller gives us innumerable delightful anecdotes about composers, singers, pianists and other artists of the past and present time, from Biblical times to "Be-bop" and "Cool".

Parents will find Mr. Waller's advice on children—and how to introduce them to music—particularly helpful. He assures us that music—at least as a pleasurable personal hobby—is a skill anyone can acquire and enjoy. And the understanding teacher can easily pass on a profound love of music, introducing young people to one of life's great pleasures.

From the experiences of my own lifetime, spent on the fringes of music, I can testify to the excellence of this book, its value as a guide and the joy it brings to the reader. I cannot play the piano or any other instrument. (My family could not afford to continue music lessons for me after the 50 cents they spent on the one and only half-hour I ever spent with a teacher.) Yet through a somewhat fortunate series of circumstances I have found myself as successively a member of the boards of two orchestras, vice-chairman of the Royal Conservatory of Music, one of the founders and later president of the Canadian Opera Company and chairman of the Music Committee of the Stratford Shakespearean Festival of Canada.

All I knew about music was that I loved it and absorbed it with enthusiasm as a member of the listening audience from the days of Louise Homer, Sergei Rachmaninoff, Edward Johnson, Ignace Paderewski, Victor Herbert and the San Carlo Opera Company right up to the present day. Music has been a nourishing part of my life as indeed it has been for many laymen. But how much richer would the experience have been if I had had this little book to read, with all its explanations of what it was and who it was that I was listening to.

Adrian Waller's Guide to Music is a wonderfully satisfying little book, whether for adults or children, for professionals or laymen. It will help its readers to endow their lives with aesthetic interest; with the enjoyment of the sensuous beauty that is the essence of music.

FLOYD S. CHALMERS
Chancellor's Office
York University, Toronto

INTRODUCTION

Most music available today was written over the past four hundred years. In the Renaissance men picked tunes on lutes. Today they are creating compositions with electronics—an expression of the machine age. Between these landmarks there emerged an enormous volume of music for every occasion imaginable.

Unfortunately, the average person has heard only a small percentage of our total musical wealth. He is generally content to confine his listening to radio and a small collection of recordings. He may not even realize what he is missing, and if he does he may have the mistaken impression that much music is beyond him.

This book is dedicated to the philosophy that music is for everyone.

Music is not an intellectual pastime, but an emotional one; its joys will never be discovered solely by reading a book. Music involves listening, and listening is an art harder to acquire than people think.

The fact that most men in the twentieth century have a listening span of less than three minutes is largely due to commercial radio, which has as its prime function the advertising without which it could not exist. As a result, an insidious pattern has evolved over the years: the music is interrupted every few minutes by a disc jockey or announcer who reads the advertisements.

Under such a system, much beautiful music is ruled out for radio by virtue of its length. The masterful composers wrote musical units of widely varying duration, but only a few overtures and some songs are short enough for commercial radio presentation. Certainly a symphony, concerto or sonata would be out of the question. Depending upon the age in which it was written, and by whom, the performance of one of these could take between five and thirty-five minutes. Thus you may be left with this ironic thought: that radio, invented in 1895, may well have killed the very thing for which it was intended—listening!

Only when we have learned to listen for more than three minutes at a time will the full enjoyment of music be ours. No one has yet been able to tell us how to do this, other than to offer the all-too-easy advice: "Close your eyes and listen," or "Try to imagine yourself on an island." One thing is certain, however; the ability to listen intelligently and with appreciation *can* be developed with practice. Some people, who have an in-born feeling for music, will extend their listening span easily. Others will have to persevere.

There are a few basic rules that are helpful in developing an appreciation of music:

- Stay with the music for as long as possible, allowing the mind to wander and return to the melody at will.
- Listen to what is beneath the melody—the contributions of other instruments that may be providing the harmony.
- Allow the music to create pictures in the mind.
- Try to decide what the composer had in his mind when he created the music.
- Beat time to the music, or move to it.
- Notice that the tempo may change in places.
- Try to comprehend the historical backcloth against which the music was originally set.
- Listen to as much music as possible.

These simple measures may not provide all the answers but they should help you listen for longer periods without becoming bored or restless. The important thing is to ride with the music—not fight it.

You might ask, "If it entails so much effort to enjoy music to the full, why bother?" The answer to that is, "Because it's *worth* the effort." Music is one of man's basic needs. It evokes emotional responses in him, stimulates his senses, and in every way enriches his life.

The fact that there is such a variety of music available makes it possible for people to choose music to suit their need at any given time. If a person is in the mood for stirring, uplifting music, he can turn to Beethoven; if he fancies romantic music, he can listen to Chopin; if he feels inclined for something more lively, there is jazz. The more he knows about music the wider his range of selection, and the greater his satisfaction.

Certainly there is a world of music to choose from. You do not have to be French to understand the impressionism of Debussy; you need not be German to appreciate Wagner. Music is international. And the enjoyment of music is a great unifying force. Your favourite pianist could be German, Russian or Chinese. And your enthusiasm for his work could be shared by the Italian grocer or the Japanese dry-cleaner.

Most of us like music in some form or another, but for different reasons. Often we enjoy a melody because we associate it with something—a person, place or event in our lives. An eminent musicologist who appreciates Bach, Handel, Mozart, Beethoven, Berlioz, Wagner and Richard Strauss, may also enjoy "Can I Canoe You Down the River?" because it reminds him of his courting days. He will not compare the piece with the masterworks; he will realize that the man who wrote "Can I Canoe You Down the River?" was not trying to dethrone any of the great composers, but merely producing a catchy song.

Many people who claim to like music, however, merely hear it; they do not *listen* to it. Music, these days, is frequently foisted upon us—sometimes when we don't even want it—in hotel lobbies, elevators, supermarkets and offices. Usually we are aware that the music is playing but we don't pay much attention to it, because it makes no emotional demands upon us. Music to which we really listen, on the other hand, is immeasurably more gratifying. For one thing, it is music that we have selected because it fills a particular need. For another, it is generally music of a different calibre than the "canned" type—less shallow and more reflective of basic human values. It gives us more nourishment for the spirit.

Without knowing it, we sometimes allow others to select our music for us. So far as commercial radio is concerned, the dangers are obvious. First, there is the chance that a disc jockey may prefer to play a recording of Mantovani and His Orchestra playing a Viennese waltz instead of the Vienna Philharmonic. Second, there is the tendency of radio stations to offer a varied choice within a small range of musical styles. Speak to the station manager some time and he will probably tell you that music comes in three stock brands: classical, middle-of-the-road, and Pop. The classification is ridiculous, because what is middle-of-the-road to one person may not be middle-of-the-road to another. Moreover, the term "classical" is incorrectly used in that sense. Classical music belongs to a mere eighty years or so at the end of the eighteenth century, a period Haydn and Mozart made their own. Like their contemporaries, they wrote music in a rigid and traditional form. It is wrong to use the word "classical" in any other way.

Another obstacle that must be overcome if a true appreciation of music is to be achieved, is the tendency to adhere to preconceived ideas. For example, many people suffer from the delusion that anything written before the second half of the twentieth century is dull. They label it "highbrow" and think they will never grow to enjoy it. The irony of this is that they are probably already quite familiar with some of this music. They have heard it in "popular" adaptations over the radio, in hotel lobbies, in the movies. They perhaps whistle the tunes. But they may never have heard the compositions played as the composer intended.

Perhaps present-day listeners are deterred by the unimaginative titles some of the composers selected. Who, unless he had already heard it, would travel downtown on a snowy night to hear a piece of music called *Toccata and Fugue in D Minor*? Yet this work, one of Bach's boldest masterpieces, has been used frequently as a musical backdrop for movies, and whether they know it or not, is familiar to many people. So we must say to ourselves, "What's in a name?" and give the music an opportunity to speak for itself.

One of the questions I am often asked is, "Where do you start in learning to appreciate music?" The answer varies from person to person. First, it is necessary to dispel the notion that because someone is without technical training in music he cannot learn to enjoy it. Obviously, training is an advantage, but a lack of it should never discourage anyone from trying to listen to music intelligently. If a person hears a work that appeals to him, he should read about it: the notes on the record jacket, the concert programme notes, an article in an encyclopaedia, or a book about the composer.

The history of music opens the door to new understanding. It is interesting to know that Beethoven wrote some of his best works while under the strain of deafness, and it is important to realize that although only fifty years separated Beethoven's first works from Bach's last, there was a world of difference in their outlook and approach.

The learner would also benefit by reading something about the structure of music. It might be helpful for him to know a little about the various types of vocal music (operas, oratorio and lieder), about instrumental music (sonatas, concertos, symphonies, operatic overtures, suites). Some knowledge of musical time would be useful—that a waltz has a steady beat of 1-2-3, 1-2-3, while a march has a beat of 1-2-3-4, 1-2-3-4, for example.

The relationship of melody and rhythm is important, too. Usually, rhythm and melody go hand in hand with equal importance and equal accent. Occasionally, though, melody is subservient to rhythm. An excellent example of this is Maurice Ravel's most famous work—the one he personally liked the least of all, "Bolero." If you listen to it, you'll see that it is nothing more than eighteen repetitions of the same theme moving with increased volume and slightly increased tempo. Towards the end there are some brazen, jazz-like interjections from some of the wind instruments, and then a crashing finale. It is, of course, a dance. Ravel himself originally called it a *dance lascive* (lewd dance), and brushed it off lightly by saying it was a musical joke—"orchestral effects without music." It came as a shock to audiences, though, when it was first danced by Ida Rubinstein at the Paris Opera on November 20, 1928. A woman was said to have called out, "Help, a madman!" Ravel himself was amazed at the success of this work, and in reply to congratulations said, "Oh, it's only a fashion."

In time, as he acquires an insight into the structure of the music and the intent of the composer, the listener should become quite discerning. It is to be hoped that he will eventually become sufficiently so to prefer Mozart's *Symphony No. 40* played as Mozart would have wanted it to a "jazzed up" version of the work. Perhaps he will even prefer to hear Schubert's glorious little songs sung in their original style rather than rendered in tasteless pomp by full orchestra.

It is true, of course, that some music has been expertly modernized, and the music lover should recognize this too. But if the listener has a real appreciation of music he will realize that we owe the composer the preservation of music in its original form and shape; there must be times when his music is performed unaltered—and certainly unmutilated.

ADRIAN WALLER

Montreal
March, 1973

ADRIAN
WALLER'S
GUIDE
TO
MUSIC

The birth of music

(1) *its origins and attributes,the Greek and Roman periods,influence of the Christian Church, the Romanesque period,the Gothic period,the Renaissance*

Just as painters, architects and writers have been conditioned by the styles and tastes of the age in which they lived, so have musicians. Their work has been fashioned out of war and peace, poverty and affluence. In fact, nearly all the important historical landmarks have left some kind of imprint on music.

Once, music reflected only a divine reverence for the Church. Today, though, man lives beneath the constant threat of nuclear war and the pressures of a technological society. He has made his music speak accordingly—live with a sense of fear and strain. On the one hand, his music throbs with a yearning to experience new things; on the other, it cries out for love, peace and personal acclamation. Music, then, continues to express not only man's thoughts, but his inner feelings and environment as well.

The precise origins of music are shrouded in as

much mystery as the beginnings of the human race. Only from legends, myths and cave drawings do we know about man's earliest attempts to express himself musically. We conjecture that he probably did this by clapping his hands and stamping his feet long before he had even learned to speak, thus developing something inherent in most of us—a sense of rhythm. What we do know more positively, however, is that music once had incredible power and was used by magicians in ancient times to exhort evil spirits. Supernatural abilities were attributed to various instruments. In the Old Testament, for example, we are told that the walls of Jericho were demolished by the blasts of trumpets. And according to writings of ancient India, the people of Bengal were once saved from famine by the voice of a singer.

Music had other uses, too. In ancient Egypt, the priest-doctors had a favourite incantation which purported to have favourable effects on the fertility of women. This incantation, called "psyche of the soul," is four thousand years old and is still preserved in the most ancient of Egyptian papyri. There are also recorded instances in which the ancient Hebrews used music to cure both physical and mental illness. The most famous recorded case, perhaps, is that of King Saul. He asked for continuous music to prevent the disintegration of his mind.

Confucius saw value in music, too. He believed it was a definite aid to harmonious living, and his theory was taken up by the early Greeks who generally regarded music as an "imitative" art—an art capable of "imitating" moral qualities and conveying them to the listener. This gave music a natural place in the education of youth. In the ideal state of the Greek philosopher Plato (429-347 B.C.), music guided young people to spiritual beauty and harmony—qualities which manifested themselves in very early Grecian architecture and sculpture.

One of Plato's pupils, the philosopher Aristotle (383-320 B.C.), developed the ideas of his teacher. He claimed that music could heal mental sickness by intensifying the effects of the illness through an excitatory melody until a state of ecstasy was attained. This, he said, would produce a kind of spiritual redemption, eventually restoring mental stability. But Aristotle also recognized music as a form of entertainment—a relaxing element after a hard day's work.

In those early days, the Greeks composed music

with a melody line for one voice, and its performance was closely linked to the poetry used in temples and arenas to accompany dancers. At the Olympic Games, the Pythian Games at Delphi, and other sports festivals where there were performances of traditional national poems, it was cultivated even more.

Few traces of early Greek music remain, but the acoustic theories of the Greeks have proved of great importance, and the scientist Pythagoras (582-500 B.C.) made physical and mathematical studies of tone intervals. In turn, these provided the basis for the theoretical research of a Roman, Boethius (c. A.D. 500), and the musicians of the Middle Ages.

The Romans inherited the musical culture of the Greeks but did not see fit to develop it further. They generally regarded music purely as an entertainment, an attitude which caused it to stagnate, so that it remained on a one-voice level until the eleventh century. It was only in the field of melody that new forms developed.

The singing at early Christian ceremonies was closely related to the ritualistic songs of the Jews—a free improvisation, with typically Oriental richness of tone and considerable use of chromaticism in the melodies. This seemed to suit the ecstatic state of mind of the early Christians, and the chief demand made upon ecclesiastical music for some time was that it should be dignified and in harmony with religious ceremony.

Augustine (345-430), one of the fathers of the Church, maintained there was a secret relationship between tones and emotions. "The sacred works prepare our souls for devotion in greater measure when they are sung than when they are spoken," he concluded. From that time on, a great deal of music was written for the Church, which, by about the seventh century, had become a powerful authority.

During the next four centuries many stylistic forms in both music and architecture evolved. The most important of these was the Romanesque style which was typified by solid, austere buildings and clear, tranquil Church music which spoke of trust in authority. It was during this period that there appeared the first traces of polyphonic music. In this type of composition two or more voices pursue a parallel theme at a fixed interval, or one voice remains constant while another moves about at varying intervals.

By the eleventh century, the Romanesque style was displaced by the Gothic. Men who had bowed humbly, with a feeling of helplessness in the presence of the divinity, now lifted their faces towards the skies. All the arts gained life and movement. Emotions found an outlet in an ecstatically joyful attempt to free matter from the weight that prevented it from rising towards the infinite. The slender pillars and light construction of the Gothic churches, with their lacework of pointed, soaring arches, gave expression to the upward aspirations of human thought. With this came choirs and the introduction of instruments. Harmony was created by having two or more distinct tunes run simultaneously—a technique we now call counterpoint. Music took on new dimensions and proportions; it needed both to fill the wide-open spaces of a new era.

Although the Netherlands eventually became the centre of musical development, Paris, with its university and famous singing school, The School of Notre Dame, was also considered important. At the university, for instance, the theory of music as we know it today was devised; the familiar system of notation was invented. Counterpoint was also developed enthusiastically, and professors at the singing school once took a simple Gregorian chant and gave it thirty-six different vocal parts.

Gregorian chant (sometimes called plainsong) was used for liturgical purposes in the Roman Catholic Church. It consisted of one unison melody, and was sung without accompaniment. These chants are still occasionally sung in the Church. Listen to them and you will notice that they do not have any set time—3/4 or 4/4 for example. The music follows, instead, the rhythm of the words, which, at the time of their appearance, were considered more important than the melody. In effect, this is why the musicians of The School of Notre Dame discarded their thirty-six-part Gregorian chant. They confessed that the intricate harmony made it impossible to comprehend the words. Choirs were subsequently given fewer harmonic parts (usually no more than eight), and any further harmony required by a composer was usually written for instrumentalists.

The Gregorian chant (probably named after Pope Gregory the Great, though some musicologists believe that it originated later) has survived in its original form. Another of its characteristics is that, unlike most music, it is without a key and is found, instead, in any one of eight modes—a system of scales used in medieval times.

In the music of the Gregorian age there is much of

4

the joy of experiment and discovery. But one of the most rapid developments of music came between 1450 and 1600. This age is known as the Renaissance and its very name indicates the essence of a new era—a rebirth. It was a notable characteristic of this period that non-clerical elements came to the fore. A well-to-do middle class was created by trade and industry and, through a rise in affluence, the princes gained greater powers with which to assert themselves politically and culturally against the Church. There was a revival of interest in ancient art and literature. In architecture, the upward aspirations of the Gothic were replaced by breadth and straight lines in clear and quiet proportions. The emphasis in painting was transferred to the human in nature, and artists looked for beauty in character, in clarity, and in logical construction. There was a reaction against the harsh realism of the Late Gothic, the favourite motifs of which were suffering and death.

Music then strove to express the true feelings and passions of ordinary people, just as it does today. The watchword of the Renaissance musician was *Dare spirito vivo alle parole* (To give the words a living spirit), and out of this came the most cultivated form of choral music this far—the madrigal. Usually written in three, four, or five parts, the madrigal provides a perfect example of counterpoint, because the melodies run simultaneously but independently, often weaving in and out and across each other. Originally, just one singer sang each part, but now these beautiful old songs are sung by full choirs especially formed to perform them in the style and costumes of their time.

Through the Renaissance, musicians sought to make music a more sophisticated art. The great achievement of Palestrina, the foremost composer of the Roman Catholic Church, was to create the tranquillity and unity that the masters of the Netherlands and France had failed to produce. This important musical figure was born around 1525 and died in Rome in 1594. His true name was Giovanni Pierluigi Sante, but because he entered the world in Palestrina, near Rome, he was simply called "da Palestrina." Little is known of his childhood, except that he earned his living as a church singer and later became an organist. His important contribution to music is that he led colleague composers in one common aim—to unify and harmonize the voice.

5

Other musicians of this era include:

William Byrd (1543-1623): English. Organist. Acclaimed as the greatest English composer of church music. Founder of the English school of madrigals. Died wealthy, having been given a monopoly of printing and selling music by Queen Elizabeth I.

John Dowland (1563-1626): English. A fine lute player and singer. Composed about one hundred songs. Went to Paris at seventeen to serve the English ambassador as a resident musician. While there became Roman Catholic. Returned to England and became Protestant again. Died relatively wealthy.

Jacopo Peri (1561-1633): Italian. From a noble family. Called "Il Zazzerino"—"the Long-Haired." Court conductor. Intensely interested in Greek mythology. Used Greek themes for some of the earliest operas known. Sang in some himself.

Thomas Morley (1557-1602): English. Studied under Byrd. Was organist at St. Paul's Cathedral. A friend of William Shakespeare. Set some of Shakespeare's songs to music, including "It Was a Lover and His Lass." Fine composer of madrigals. Also given a monopoly of music printing and selling by the Queen. Died wealthy.

Guillaume Dufay (some time before 1400-1474): Flemish. Started his career as a cathedral choirboy. Later took religious instruction and became a canon. Wrote mainly for the Church.

Michael Praetorius (1571-1621): German. Real name: Schulz. Cathedral organist and early conductor. Wrote mostly for the Church. Some dance music. Also wrote a history of music.

Orlando Lasso (1530-1594): Flemish. As a boy sang for foreign nobles. Travelled widely through France and Italy. Wrote German-style religious works while the Court music-master in Munich. Considered the last and greatest of the Flemish school. Died reasonably wealthy.

Thomas Tallis (1505-1585): English. Organist. Friend of Byrd and almost as influential. Shared Byrd's exclusive rights. Died wealthy.

6

By the sixteenth century, England was developing instrumental music alongside the madrigal. Elsewhere in Europe, too, instruments were being used more independently, though there were few instrumental compositions other than variations on well-known songs. Purely instrumental forms, however, were already making their appearances, particularly in organ and lute music.

The Renaissance also saw the birth of opera and ballet. Peri's *Dafne*, said to be the first opera ever written, was performed only once and privately in the home of Count Bardi in Florence in 1597. On the strength of it, Peri was commissioned to write another, *Euridice*, to celebrate the wedding, in 1600, of Henry IV of France and Maria de Medici. Some years before this, in 1581, the French Court under Catherine de Medici, had witnessed the birth of ballet. When a troupe of dancers arrived to entertain the Queen with a work called *Ballet Comique de la Reine*, ballet was developed immediately; opera, on the other hand, had to wait about one hundred years to begin development as a performing art. Nothing, however, better reflects the spirit and forward thrust of the Renaissance than these two illustrious beginnings.

Suggested Listening:

Palestrina:	*Missa Papae Marcelli, Missa Brevis, Magnificat*
Tallis:	*Lamentations of Jeremiah*
Morley:	Elizabethan madrigals, ayres, harpsichord pieces

7

The Baroque and Classical periods

(2) *composers and highlights of the Baroque period, Rococo music, composers and highlights of the Classical period*

After the Renaissance came the Baroque period. It started roughly around the beginning of the seventeenth century and ended with the death of George Frideric Handel in 1759. Some musicologists, however, hold that this exceedingly fertile era in musical history (primarily for opera and instrumental music) ended nine years earlier, in 1750—upon the death of its most prolific master, Johann Sebastian Bach. But unless you intend making a more diligent historical study, that is of little importance. Bach and Handel were born within a month of each other and, although each had distinctive musical traits, their work bore characteristics typical of their time. They have since been pronounced so significant as to suggest that if their music could be removed from the Baroque period, little would be left other than a huge deluge of vivacious, decorative violin music and an even bigger collection of arias.

Johann Sebastian Bach (1685-1750): German. Happy childhood. Choirboy. Studied violin and viola under his father's direction. Orphaned before eleven. Taken into home by his brother, Johann Christoph, who taught him music. Twenty children from two marriages. First wife was his cousin. Second wife was Anna Magdalena, for whom Bach wrote clavier works and songs. Went blind in 1749. Unappreciated in his time. Death not even mentioned in official publications or newspapers. Last work dictated to his son-in-law from his deathbed.

George Frideric Handel (1685-1759): English. Naturalized. Originally German. Appointed assistant cathedral organist at twelve. Four years later, senior organist. Money from this met his lodging expenses while studying law. Later went to England. Wrote an opera in fourteen days and received a life pension from Queen Anne. Pension later increased by George I. Very prolific. Forty-six operas, thirty-two oratorios and many works for orchestra. Went blind. Conducted and played from memory. Died seven years later. Never married. Loved and honoured. Buried in Westminster Abbey.

While many of the Renaissance composers are affectionately remembered as diligent craftsmen, Bach and Handel emerge as artists. They mastered the craft they had inherited and added so much creative genius that the craft became an art. The difference can be likened to the conscientious craftsman jeweller who conforms to reliable, popular patterns and the artist-jeweller who, having thoroughly acquainted himself with his craft, has progressed creatively so that every ring he makes is a work of art, bearing his own inimitable mark.

The character of Baroque music is best summed up by the definition of the word "baroque." This was borrowed from the Portuguese word *barroco*, which means a highly ornamental, irregularly-shaped pearl. The French word *baroque* was first used to describe aptly a highly-ornamental style of architecture and decoration fashionable throughout Europe, particularly in Italy, in the early eighteenth and nineteenth centuries. Musicologists later borrowed it to define music of the same period—music which became decorative and ornamental as a distinct reaction against the classical, straight lines of the Renaissance. This music expresses a search for life, movement and power.

Many extraordinarily prolific composers belong to

the Baroque period (a list would more aptly resemble the New York telephone directory than a chapter in a book), and many of these, like Bach and Handel, were German. In terms of collective output, though, the age really belongs to the Italians, of whom Antonio Vivaldi (1675-1741), an incorrigible concerto writer, was unquestionably one of the most industrious. Apart from his popular *Four Seasons* (four concertos depicting the seasons of the year), Vivaldi composed about five hundred similar works for almost every instrument you can think of, including the bassoon, piccolo, trumpet, oboe, mandolin and violin. The two most important Baroque writers for the violin, however, were Arcangelo Corelli (1653-1713) and Francesco Geminiani (1687-1762). But this is not hard to understand. Both were violinists. In fact, Corelli was Geminiani's teacher.

Giuseppe Tartini (1692-1770) also wrote busily for the violin. He was considered the greatest violinist of his day, although he originally studied for the priesthood, then switched to law and later decided to become an officer in the army. During this time, he studied music and became more and more interested in being a violinist and teacher. But his career was temporarily interrupted when he married against the wishes of his wife's guardian, Cardinal Cornaro. The Cardinal ordered Tartini's arrest. Tartini's family cut off all support and the young composer was forced to flee to a monastery in Assisi where the monks protected him while he remained in hiding until 1715. In the monastery, Tartini perfected his violin playing and improved the violin bow, and by the time he was pardoned he was already famous.

Among the most productive writers for the clavier, an early edition of the piano, were François Couperin (1668-1733), a Frenchman, and another Italian, Domenico Scarlatti (1685-1757). Domenico was the son of Alessandro Scarlatti (1660-1725). He wrote one hundred and fifty oratorios, around six hundred cantatas, chamber music and many pieces for the clavier. A. Scarlatti, however, is chiefly remembered for his influence on the development of opera; he composed more than one hundred of them.

Other important opera composers of the Baroque period were Francesco Durante (1684-1755), Baldassare Galuppi (1706-1785), Leonardo Leo (1694-1744) and Giovanni Battista Pergolesi (1710-1736). Pergolesi's themes were used in this century in adaptations by the late Igor Stravinsky.

Johann Sebastian Bach, one of the most important composers of all time, bequeathed to posterity the fugue and the toccata, and a flood of fine music for the keyboard. Like his friend Handel, Bach went blind. Unlike Handel, however, he was not appreciated in his day.

10

Jean-Philippe Rameau (1683-1764), another Frenchman, emerges as a significant Baroque writer, too. He wrote many early French operas and, like most of his counterparts, some lively works for various instruments. But Rameau's significance is twofold; he is noted for his work as a theorist and for pioneering the Baroque influence in French music. Rameau, in fact, had studied with the Italians. When he decided he did not like Italian ways, he returned to France to teach music and play the organ in a church in Avignon, and took the decorative Baroque trend with him.

In much the same way Heinrich Schutz (1585-1672), a German, and Dietrich Buxtehude (1637-1707), a Danish composer, helped stamp Italian ways on other parts of Europe. And to a certain extent, even though he had a style all his own, Handel espoused Italian writing. He went to Italy for three years in 1706 at the age of twenty-one, and there received much of his musical education.

George Frideric Handel, a prolific opera writer, also conducted, and played the organ from memory. Queen Anne and King George both granted him life pensions, thus enabling Handel to live comfortably in England, his adopted country.

The Baroque period in music is typified by vitality and pulse. Young people today call that pulse "beat" and think it is something new. It isn't. Listen to the driving force behind much of the music of this age (admittedly much of it sounds alike) and decide for yourself. Bach has "pulse," too. This, and his superbly inventive structures have made his music almost indestructible, even when it is subjected to musical instruments about which he knew absolutely nothing—the piano, the electric guitar, the electronic synthesizer or Moog, to name just a few.

Apart from being extremely fertile in terms of musical output, the Baroque era produced many musical forms, both for the voice and instruments. These are either still used today or have led to other, more advanced forms. Some of these are:

Oratorio: A large religious work written for soloists, chorus, orchestras, and sometimes an organ. Unlike opera, it is not staged. It differs, therefore, only in terms of presentation. Some of the most famous of all oratorios are Haydn's *The Creation* and *The Seasons*, Handel's *Messiah*, Mendelssohn's *St. Paul* and *Elijah*, Berlioz' *L'Enfance du Christ*, and César Franck's *Béatitudes*. Some important oratorios composed during the twentieth century are Elgar's *The Dream of Gerontius*,

11

Walton's *Belshazzar's Feast*, Honegger's *King David*, and Stravinsky's opera-oratorio *Oedipus Rex*.

The aria: Aria is the Italian word for "air." Arias can be likened to long, important speeches in a play. They are sung in operas and oratorios by the principal singers or characters.

Recitative: This term comes from the Latin word *recitare*, which means "to recite." A recitative is usually delivered in a speech-like form of singing and invariably precedes an aria or song in an opera or oratorio.

Concerto: Concerto is an Italian word meaning "concert." We have come to know a concerto as a work for a solo instrument and orchestra—or a group of solo instruments and orchestra, though this is less common. The forerunner to the concerto was invented in the Baroque period and was called a *concerto grosso* ("great concert"). It was written for larger groups of instruments with a full orchestra behind them. Examples of the modern reference to a concerto in which a solo instrument is pitted against an orchestra are Beethoven's very powerful *Violin Concerto*, Tchaikovsky's *First Piano Concerto*, and any one of Mozart's twenty-seven piano concertos. However, Mozart also wrote some concertos for two pianos.

Fugue: A fugue is said to be the most exacting of all musical forms. It derives its name from the Latin word *fuga*, which means "flight." It is an apt description. The music tends to fly along horizontally according to certain principles of imitative counterpoint (that is, two or more distinct melodies running together to make "musical sense"). The fugue, however, is much more complicated than most contrapuntal forms. It can have as many as five parts woven together, though they do not necessarily start or finish together. The different melodies also imitate and answer each other. Perhaps this diagram of a four-part progression will help explain:

Soprano: One line of music states a theme that goes on and on . . . .

Contralto: A second "voice" then restates the theme or "answers" . . . .

Tenor: A third line enters with the original theme . . . .

Bass: A fourth line "answers" again and joins in . . . .

12

So complicated a form is the fugue that it has been the subject of several books. It is impossible, therefore, to enter into much more detail in a book of this size and nature.

Toccata: A toccata comes from the Italian word *toccare*, meaning "touched." It is simply an instrumental piece designed to show the skill of the artist. J.S. Bach wrote magnificent toccatas for both organ and clavier, and other more recent composers have obliged artists with the same form for various instruments, particularly the piano.

❖   ❖   ❖   ❖

Towards the end of the Baroque period, styles began to change and there began a brief but fashionable style of music called Rococo. "Rococo," another term borrowed from art history, describes music written between 1710 and about 1775, when a kind of elegant and luxurious decoration was stylish. During this period music was characterized by a lightness and frivolity quite different from the relative seriousness of the earlier Baroque. The designation "gallant style" is often used to describe it. The period generally depicted the cultivation of the pleasures of life and joy, and most Rococo music was composed for the sole entertainment of the court and nobility. Its favourite forms were the divertimento and the serenade.

Divertimento is an Italian word meaning "amusement" or "recreation." Musically speaking, then, a divertimento is a work light in character, written for instrumental groups and performed for nothing more than its entertainment value. A famous example is the well-known *Eine kleine Nachtmusik* by Wolfgang Amadeus Mozart (1756-1791), who used the divertimento form frequently. Mozart was also fond of using the serenade which is, generally speaking, a song sung by a young man to his sweetheart. The definition has been distorted, though, and many serenades have been written more recently for instrumental ensembles rather than just the voice.

Composers whose music is most typical of the Rococo or the gallant style are:

François Couperin (1668-1733): French. Best-known

13

member of a large family of musicians who played the organ at the Church of St. Gervais for two hundred years. Was influenced by Corelli. In turn, influenced J.S. Bach. Wrote a book on how to play the harpsichord. Wrote more than two hundred harpsichord pieces. Taught by his father.

Georg Philipp Telemann (1681-1767): German. Originally studied law. Eminence in music came later through self-study. Extremely prolific. Organist, too. Music is facile but shallow. Some of his instrumental works recently given new life, especially those written for the flute and recorder.

Carl Philipp Emanuel Bach (1714-1788): German. Second son of J.S. Bach's first marriage. Studied law. Later turned to music. Became court harpsichord player to Frederick the Great in Berlin. Succeeded Telemann as director of church music in Hamburg. Wrote a book on playing the harpsichord. Great influence on Haydn.

Apart from Mozart, his friend Joseph Haydn (1732-1809) also used the Rococo style. This bridges the Baroque period with the infinitely less productive Classical period in which Mozart and Haydn really belong.

Generally speaking, the Classicists, of whom Haydn and Mozart were the busiest, were dedicated to developing musical forms inherited from Baroque composers, rather than creating new ones. They quickly abandoned the abrupt loud and soft contrasts of typical Baroque music (clearly evident in the early passages of Vivaldi's *The Four Seasons*) and diffused them into a wide range of more gentle shadings in volume. They also found that pauses could be used for dramatic effect (as is evident in the first movement of Mozart's *Symphony No. 41, Jupiter*), and that special moods or tonal colours could be attained by sustaining a particularly crucial tone.

Some of these new musical devices and statements were not considered pleasurable to all listeners, and Frederick the Great predicted that because of them music would one day disappear.

Although the first signs of Classicism emerged as Bach and Handel were bringing the Baroque style to its culmination, it did not really begin to take firm root

14

until around 1740. And it ended relatively quickly, early in the nineteenth century. Classicism's fundamental concepts were organic unity and monumental simplicity, which suggests that it may well have sprung up in opposition to the Rococo period, which, under Louis XV, was frivolous, lighthearted and, to some degree, amoral.

Christoph Willibrand Gluck (1714-1787) was one of the first to bring the Classical elements to the fore by a diligent and thorough restructuring of musical form. This is particularly evident in his operas, which were his main interest. More than this, though, Gluck typified the predominantly German influence of the Classical age. This found music moving parallel to the Classical literature of the writer Johann Wolfgang von Goethe (1749-1832).

Perhaps the era's most cherished gift to music is the classical sonata which, though born in the Baroque era, had to wait for men with the capabilities of Haydn and Mozart before it could be developed further. Haydn and Mozart used the sonata widely and, true to the philosophy of Classicism, bestowed upon it so much shape and dignity that today it is considered the most powerful and perfect form in all instrumental music.

Largely through this studious work, the supremely inventive Mozart and Haydn made the Classical period virtually their own.

A sonata is a composition in several "sections" for one or two instruments. There are piano sonatas, violin sonatas, cello sonatas, and so on. The term was used as far back as 1616, although Johann Kuhnau (1660-1722), one of the less significant Baroque composers, is thought to have written the first examples with a series of short pieces for the harpsichord. (These were later called the Biblical Sonatas.) In those days, that was exactly what a sonata was—a short piece in one section. Had it been sung, it would have been a cantata. (The word *sonata* is Italian for "sounded"; *cantata* means "sung.")

Haydn and Mozart, and later Beethoven, decided to break the sonata into sections which we now know as movements. Each movement in such a work is usually a self-contained piece, though not necessarily independent of the others. The Classical conception was to attain variety by altering the pace of these movements so that a slow one was followed by another, faster one, thus helping the full work to retain its interest.

Another form of music divided into movements is the symphony, the development of which can be

15

attributed directly to the evolution of the sonata. The symphony, in fact, is nothing more than a sonata for the orchestra. It is a valuable gift from the Classical period.

Had it not been for Haydn, the symphony as we know it today might never have come about. Haydn, whose gay, light-hearted personality is reflected in his music, wrote more than one hundred symphonies, the early ones of which were in three movements. Mozart, on the other hand, wrote only forty-one symphonies. But his were usually longer compositions than those of his contemporaries, sometimes consisting of four movements.

Probably no composer had such a fertile imagination and left such a large legacy of music as Mozart. His work was endowed with that special grace, that ease of expression which encompasses everything man has ever felt about either this world or the next. Born the son of a Salzburg violinist and assistant Kapellmeister of considerable skill, Mozart was, perhaps, the most outstanding infant prodigy ever known. He began composing at six and never stopped in a career of just less than thirty years.

He had everything—the most natural gift, the most fluent style, an incredible command of every instrument in his orchestra and an exuberance of spirit no one has yet been able to emulate. He was also the greatest concert pianist of his day, a formidable violinist, and an outstanding organist. No wonder legends pursue him— and some are true! How many composers could write a masterpiece like the overture to the opera *Don Giovanni* in a single night so that the players in the pit could rehearse it in the morning with the ink barely dry? Who else could have written in six weeks works of such supreme quality as Mozart's last three symphonies, or twelve splendidly eloquent piano concertos between 1784 and 1786, pausing in between to compose another operatic triumph—*The Marriage of Figaro*?

The secret was simple enough. Mozart first worked everything out in his head, then wrote it down quickly so that it retained its shine and spontaneity. Virtually everything he produced bore this trait, and he composed more and better music than anyone had ever done before—or since. Yet when he died of a kidney ailment at only thirty-five, he was given a pauper's funeral, so meagre were the funds provided by his patron.

In comparison with the fertility of the previous era

Wolfgang Amadeus Mozart, the most outstanding infant prodigy ever known, began composing at the age of six and never stopped during his short lifetime. His gift was natural, his style fluent, and he left us a wealth of eloquent music.

16

there were few Classical composers, but they made up in quality what they lacked in numbers. Beside Mozart, the principal figures were:

Franz Joseph Haydn (1732-1809): Austrian. Exceptionally prolific. Composed more than one hundred symphonies. Very unhappy in a childless marriage. Nevertheless, gay, light-hearted, sober, sane and easily pleased. Affectionately known as "Papa." Close friend of Mozart, whose genius he admired.

Franz Joseph Haydn wrote more than one hundred symphonies, as well as a quantity of gay, light-hearted chamber music and a magnificent oratorio entitled The Creation.

Christoph Willibald Gluck (1714-1787): German. Greedy, sober and sometimes eccentric. Had his piano moved into a field so he could compose in natural surroundings. Wrote more than one hundred operas (his main strength), many of which are lost. Handel said of him: "He knows no more counterpoint than my cook."

The Classical period saw the beginning, too, of one of the finest collections of symphonies ever to be written—Beethoven's Nine Symphonies, often referred to as "the nine great monuments to music." Eight of these works are in four movements. The sixth, more often called *The Pastoral Symphony*, has five. In general, though, the number of movements in either a classical sonata or symphony varies between two and six.

With the progression of the sonata into the larger, symphonic form came the need to develop the orchestra. In effect, the Classicists did this too. Not only did they utilize new instruments, but they produced the basis of the modern symphony orchestra which, by definite and clear division, was given balance, character and efficiency. Most of this work was carried out by a group of outstanding musicians assembled by a passionate devotee of the art—the elector of Mannheim, Germany. These musicians, now more simply referred to as "the Mannheimers," displayed special technical facility and excellent ensemble playing, and endowed the existing and steadily emerging music of their time with continuity and definite expression.

But it was the capacity of their orchestra that is, perhaps, considered the more significant achievement. A contemporary writer commented poetically upon its capabilities. He wrote: "its forte is thunder; its crescendo a waterfall; its diminuendo a crystal-clear brook murmuring in the distance; its pianissimo a breath of spring."

The realization that the orchestra had symphonic potential and could be a vehicle for musical ideas fell upon Haydn and later upon Mozart. Accordingly, they enlarged the orchestra. But it was left to Ludwig van Beethoven (1770-1827) to expand the orchestra further.

Some of Beethoven's early compositions represent the rigid conservatism of the Classical period. Most, however, are very definitely a part of the next era—the Romantic period. Having been clearly influenced by Bach, Haydn and Mozart, Beethoven stood at the threshold of an age dedicated to bigger orchestras, bigger canvases—and larger sounds.

Suggested Listening:

Baroque
Rameau:	*Pièces de Clavecin*
Lully:	*Bourgeois Gentilhomme, The Triumph of Love*
Monteverdi:	*Orfeo*
Purcell:	*Dido and Aeneas, The Fairy Queen*, suites for harpsichord
J.S. Bach:	*The Great Fugue, Brandenburg Concerto No. 5*
Vivaldi:	*The Four Seasons*
Handel:	*Messiah, Water Music, Royal Fireworks Music. Arrival of the Queen of Sheba* (Julius Caesar)

Classical
Haydn:	*Symphony No. 94* ("Surprise"), *Symphony No. 101* ("Clock"), *Symphony No. 103* ("Drumroll"), *The Creation*
Mozart:	Overtures to *Marriage of Figaro* and *Don Giovanni, Eine kleine Nachtmusik, Symphony No. 3* ("Haffner"), *Symphony No. 40, Symphony No. 41* ("Jupiter"), sonatas for piano, *Clarinet Concerto*, horn concertos
Beethoven:	*Symphony No. 1, Symphony No. 2*

Romanticism

(39) *Beethoven, Berlioz and the growth of the orchestra, other composers of the Romantic period*

Beethoven's rejection of Classicism is not difficult to understand. He was considerably younger than either Mozart or Haydn, with whom he had studied, and was not nearly so deep-rooted in the eighteenth century. With his unruly, black hair swept up into a lion's mane, he belonged to a younger generation which championed the ideals of the French Revolution. He was an ardent believer in civil rights and wanted the freedom of movement Classicism could not provide. The romanticist within him was bursting to free itself.

Two hundred years after his birth, we are still wondering what kind of man Beethoven really was. He was described by his contemporaries as a short man, five feet two or three inches tall, with a round nose and an inflamed, pock-marked complexion. The same sources say that he was clumsy, vain, paranoid and unhealthy. Yet the romantic legend persists: Beethoven was a

shaggy Titan with defiant jaw, scowling brow and an indomitable will, who battled fate alone.

Perhaps there was a particular insight in Haydn's comment to Beethoven. He said: "You give me the impression of a man with several heads, several hearts and several souls." But Beethoven said of himself: "When I open my eyes I must sigh at what I see; it is contrary to my religion and I must despise the world which does not suspect that music is a higher revelation than all wisdom and philosophy. It is the wine which inspires to new creation, and I am the Bacchus who presses out this glorious wine for men . . . and makes them drunk with the spirit."

And what of inspiration? A contemporary reported that "he would not infrequently, in a fit of the most complete abstraction, go to his washbasin and pour several jugs of water upon his hands, all the while humming and roaring, for sing he could not. After dabbling in the water till his clothes were wet through, he would pace up and down the room with a vacant expression of

Ludwig van Beethoven's music is both powerful and universal, and speaks of everything for which Romanticism stands. "Freedom above all!" Beethoven said of his art. With freedom he changed the course of musical destiny.

countenance, and his eyes frightfully distended. Then he would set himself at his table and write; and afterwards get up again to the washbasin and dabble and hum as he did before. No one dared disturb him for these were his moments, or rather his hours, of profoundest meditation. It will be readily believed that the people in whose houses he lodged were not very well pleased when they found the water trickling through the floor." Indeed, the sign "Beethoven Lived Here" could legitimately be posted forty-three times around Vienna.

But he changed his servants even more frequently than he changed his apartments. Of one he wrote: "Not kindness, but fear is the only means of dealing with such people. . . . Miss Nany is quite changed since I threw half a dozen books at her; probably something of it chanced to penetrate into her brain or evil heart."

There are countless and colourful reports to show that Beethoven was not particularly good at coping with life on a personal level, but his music shows that he coped very well with it on a different plane. He was confronted with the personal calamity of deafness; he was tormented by the thought of Europe ravaged by the Napoleonic Wars; and yet he continued to create his great masterpieces. Faced with evil and grief, it was all the more essential to cherish what was noble in man. And here, indeed, was Beethoven the Titan—in defiance of fate, in affirmation of life. Beethoven wrote of himself: "I am that which is. I am all what is, what was, what will be. No mortal man has lifted my veil." We have his music—beautiful, powerful and universal. Need we ask for more?

Romanticism presents a complex picture. Basically, it begins near the first part of the nineteenth century when new classes of society were coming into power, when artists generally found it necessary to turn from the "cold" concept of formal, rigid, intellectual and precise art of their predecessors to work of a freer, imaginative and more emotional kind. Barriers fell. An increase in anxiety, aspiration and ambition was paralleled by a growing desire to escape from everyday life. Hence there was a distinctive enthusiasm for nature and everything distant—distant lands and distant times. From there, it was not too far from the land of make-believe. In music, there was appreciable freedom from the strict forms of the masterful Classical composers, greater self-expression, and a marked use of chromatic and more

In this house, in the picturesque city of Bonn, West Germany, the great Beethoven was born. Most of his composing was done in Vienna, however.

inventive and adventurous harmonies. There were also larger sounds, a fuller range of orchestral colours, new rhythmic patterns, and visionary, fantastic ideas.

The Frenchman Hector Berlioz (1803-1869) was a make-believe composer of fantastic ideas—and certainly one of the greatest figures of the Romantic movement. He wrote on a grand scale—music which could be compared with the huge canvases of the painter Eugène Delacroix and the powerful novels and poems of Victor Hugo. He read Poe and De Quincey and had an exceptionally strong feeling for the bizarre, to which his *Symphony Fantastique* bears undeniable witness.

The story of the symphony's conception is an interesting one. At twenty-four, Hector Berlioz was not only in love with the works of William Shakespeare, but with one of his interpreters, the actress Harriet Smithson, as well. When she paid him no attention, he decided to document his love and hate by putting her at the centre of a symphonic work which has since been recognized as one of the mightiest orchestral show-pieces ever composed. It tells how a musician of extreme, morbid sensibility and fervent imagination is brought to despair by love. He takes opium, seeking death, but finds only the weird visions of the drugged mind. What he now feels and recalls in the wilderness of his sick brain is expressed in music. His beloved is now a melody which haunts him everywhere. He eventually kills the girl when he believes she is unfaithful to him, is paraded to the guillotine (the music for the march is reputed to have been written overnight), and executed. But the composer has still another bizarre twist for us. The young artist is haunted even after death. His funeral is attended by an ungodly revel of demons, and the girl he killed out of love arrives as a witch.

The Romantic period is much more than Beethoven and Berlioz, though both are considered extremely important at opposite ends of the scales. Beethoven did not have Berlioz' fantastic ideas and Berlioz did not possess Beethoven's strong nationalism and patriotism— feelings that became generally dominant in this period as music once again broadened its horizons.

Other composers who can definitely be described as Romanticists are:

Felix Mendelssohn (1809-1847): German. Composed the overture to *A Midsummer Night's Dream*, perhaps his best-known work, at only seventeen. Good-natured.

Devoted to his wife and four children. Died aged thirty-eight, exhausted through constant and laborious writing and conducting. .

Robert Schumann (1810-1856): German. A friend of Brahms. Studied law, though his ambition was to become a concert pianist. Gave up the latter when he damaged his hand. Later devoted his life to composition and writing for a music magazine he launched with three friends. Married pianist Clara Wieck. Eight children. Suffered severely from depression and hallucinations. Attempted suicide. Died in an asylum aged only forty-six.

Anton Dvorak (1841-1904): Czech. Went to the United States in 1891. Fascinated by Negroes, Indians and their customs. Used their folk songs for *New World Symphony*. Married. Six children. Simple and straightforward. Called himself "a plain, Bohemian musician." Died suddenly at sixty-three.

Bedrich Smetana (1824-1884): Czech. First Czech to compose nationalistic works. Brilliant pianist. First wife was a pianist, too. Friend of Dvorak. Became totally deaf at fifty. Died in a mental home aged sixty. Best-known work is *The Bartered Bride*, an opera.

Richard Wagner (1840-1893): German. Like Mozart, worth several books. Son of a policeman. Married twice. Three children. Revolutionary. Fled to Switzerland to escape jail. Also fled from creditors. Always in financial trouble. Persistent love troubles, too. Forever seeking his ideal woman. Had many jealous lovers. Genius of the highest order. Not in the least modest. Saw himself as the world's greatest thinker, philosopher, dramatist, conductor and composer, and was probably all of these in his time. Decided that the world owed him a living. It did. Remarkably prolific. Despite being "a monster," as he has been called, he gave the world passionate, romantic music and powerful orchestrations.

Johannes Brahms (1833-1897): German. Began composing at thirteen. Started his career as a pianist in the bars of Berlin's "red light" district. Greatly encouraged by Schumann. Exceptionally generous to Schumann's family after Schumann's death. Eventually fell in love with Schumann's young widow. Affair came to nothing.

Richard Wagner owed everyone money and was despised for his morals, but he wrote musical dramas on a large scale and left us orchestrations unsurpassed for their depth of feeling. He and Giuseppe Verdi brought genius of the highest order to the latter half of the Romantic period.

His own severest critic, he destroyed everything he wrote before nineteen. Despite his affair with Mrs. Schumann, he was considered a woman-hater. Never married. Died of a liver disease.

Edvard Grieg (1843-1907): Norwegian. Began piano at six with his mother as his teacher. Already composing at nine. One of his most famous pieces, incidental music to Ibsen's *Peer Gynt*, earned him a life pension from the Norwegian government. Married a singer for whom he wrote more than 150 songs. One child. Happy marriage. Sick for the last seventeen years of his life.

Gabriel Fauré (1845-1924): French. Sixth child of a schoolmaster too poor to give son musical training. Fine organist. Deafness forced retirement.

Georges Bizet (1838-1875): French. Real name: Alexandre César Léopold. A weakling. Suffered from heart attacks from his youth. Despite all this, cheerful, straightforward, good-natured, sociable and unpretentious. Lacked a belief in his own ability. "To be a success in our time," he once wrote, "one has either to be dead or German." He was right. He was greatly underrated as a composer. His last work, the opera *Carmen* (1875), is without a doubt his most popular. He died one hour after the curtain had fallen on the thirty-first performance of *Carmen*—on his wedding anniversary. Cause of death: heart attack.

Franz Schubert (1797-1828): Austrian. Thirteenth of a family of fourteen children, of whom nine died in infancy. Genius song writer in the Romantic style, though some earlier works are distinctly classical. Proud, happy, financially poor. A bachelor and content to remain so. Had many friends who collected money to publish his early songs, including *Erlkoenig* (The Earl King). Died at thirty-one, sick and unhappy, leaving an unfinished symphony. His last wish, to be buried next to Beethoven, was granted.

Carl Maria von Weber was a fine orchestrator, but it is agreed that his most important contribution was in the field of opera.

Carl Maria von Weber (1786-1826): German. A dramatic composer and a great Romanticist. Best works: operas, of which *Der Freischuetz* and *Oberon* are the most popular. Also, two fine clarinet concertos. His title, "Baron," used in good faith, turned out to be the product of his father's imagination; no noble blood in the family. Good opera conductor. Made enemies through his overbearing personality. Married. Two children. Suffered from tuberculosis. Defied the doctor and went to London to direct *Oberon*. Died there, aged thirty-nine.

Then there was Peter Tchaikovsky (1840-1893), whose work seems to embrace everything for which Romanticism ever stood. Yet it is quite fashionable, in certain circles, to look down a patronizing nose at his music, to dismiss it as overblown and over-emotional, and to rank the creative genius low. Poor Tchaikovsky. It was not much better during his lifetime, when even at the height of his international fame, he had to dodge all manner of critical onslaughts. The fourth of his six symphonies, according to one of his learned contemporaries, is "confusion, twaddle and tittle-tattle"; his *Fifth Symphony* "sounds like a hoard of demons struggling in a torrent of brandy"; his *Sixth Symphony*, the "Pathétique," "threads all the foul ditches and sewers, as vulgar, obscene and unclean as music can be."

What, then, accounts for Tchaikovsky's being as popular with the average concert-goer as he is unpopular with the critics? Why are his concertos and symphonies loved better and played more frequently than those of almost anyone except Beethoven? Why, if it comes to that, has his music repeatedly attracted the plagiaristic attention of the makers of popular music on Broadway and Tin Pan Alley? Two full-scale musical comedies have been based on Tchaikovsky's compositions and there have been half a dozen Hit Parade tunes: "Tonight we Love" (the opening passages of his *First Piano Concerto*), "The Story of a Starry Night" (from the *Sixth Symphony*), "Moon Love" (from the *Fifth Symphony*), "On the Isle of May" (from his *Andante Cantabile*), "Our Love" (from his passionate *Romeo and Juliet* overture) and "The Things I Love" (from his *Romance in F Minor*).

I am not going to offer a convenient, neat explanation for this phenomenon, but it seems likely that beyond the obvious reason—Tchaikovsky's glowing gift for melody, his instinctive feeling for instrumental colours, and so on—lies his conception of music as a grand and glorious emotional explosion. He admitted that he would probably go to his grave without ever being able to compose a piece of music in perfect form, but he exulted in his ability to let music speak from and to the heart, rather than to the intellect.

Tchaikovsky's personal life was a morass of fears, psychoses and traumas. "He was as brittle as porcelain," his governess wrote about him when he was five or six. "A trifle wounded him deeply, and the least criticism or reproof would upset him alarmingly. I also observe that music had a great effect upon his nervous system, and after a lesson, he was invariably overwrought and excited. Once I found him sitting up in bed, with bright, feverish eyes, crying to himself. 'Oh, this music, this music,' he said. 'Save me from it. It will not give me any peace.' "

As he grew up, he was still unable to find inner peace. He remained moody, tense and inordinately shy; he added a collection of morbid fears and superstitions to his blossoming list of psychological ailments and he soon became the proud possessor of the world's most highly-developed inferiority complex. He destroyed several operas and all manner of lesser pieces because he considered them unworthy. Even when his inspiration ran highest and public enthusiasm was at its peak, he tortured himself with totally unfounded fears that his creative powers had fled. He had several nervous breakdowns, attempted suicide by standing up to his neck in the icy waters of the Neva River and gave up conducting for ten years because he was terrified that the exertions might make his head roll off his shoulders.

Ironically, less than a week after the first performance of his *Pathétique Symphony*, on October 28, 1893, Tchaikovsky died during a cholera epidemic, having ignored repeated warnings about drinking contaminated water without boiling it.

How fortunate for us all that Tchaikovsky never allowed the turmoil of his everyday affairs to interfere with his musical destiny! He worked steadily, in good times and bad, making notes in a little book he always carried with him, just as Beethoven had done before him, and carefully setting aside a specific number of hours every day for composition. When he became deeply involved with a particular piece, he would plunge into it, skipping meals and working right through sleepless nights.

There are, indeed, few better examples of the nationalistic elements in music than his *1812 Overture*, which he was commissioned in 1880 to write to celebrate the consecration of the Cathedral of the Redeemer in Moscow. The music marks the great Russian victory over Napoleon's army. In the true tradition of his era, Tchaikovsky was far more concerned with dramatic effects than form. Neither did he concern himself with the chronological order of historic events. He merely intended to create, through his music, the general impression of battle—with a prayer, the tumult of fighting, and the jubilation of victory. Napoleon's army is represented by a fanfare theme based on the "Marseillaise," the French national anthem. This is challenged and eventually overwhelmed by the hymn-like melody of the prayer with which the work opens.

More can be said about Tchaikovsky. Let it suffice, however, to say that he and his colleagues generally felt they were composing for all humanity, regarding their dependence on society as barriers to the free unfolding of their creative powers. In so doing, they needed larger, fuller orchestral sounds and a greater repertoire of adventurously harmonious effects.

Suggested Listening:

Beethoven:	*Symphony No. 6* ("Pastorale"), *Symphony No. 3* ("Eroica"), *Symphony No. 5* ("Fate"), *Piano Sonatas No. 8* ("Pathétique"), *No. 14* ("Moonlight"), *No. 21* ("Waldstein"), *Violin Concerto, The Leonore Overtures*
Schubert:	*String Quartet No. 14* ("Death and the Maiden"), *String Quintet in A* ("Trout"), *Symphony No. 8* ("Unfinished"), *Symphony No. 9* ("The Great")
Berlioz:	*Symphony Fantastique, Requiem*
Tchaikovsky:	*Symphony No. 6* ("Pathétique"), *1812 Overture, Romeo and Juliet*
Mendelssohn:	Overture to *Fingal's Cave*

The 20th Century

(4) *Impressionistic composers,*
Expressionistic composers,
composers of twelve-tone music,
the Post-Romanticists, other
important composers of the century

While Romanticism was in full bloom there appeared
another style of music—and another turning point. Impressionism, as it is called, came from other arts, particularly painting. In many ways it had the same basis as
Romanticism and sought essentially to express identical
ideas, but differently. Many foremost late-nineteenth-
century painters such as Monet, Degas and Renoir embarked on a new style of art which left details to the
imagination and which presented the subject vaguely. So
too did the Impressionistic composers. They used new
tonal harmonies and new progressions to attain the same
"misty" effect and, like their colleague painters, also
tended to suggest rather than to describe.

Claude Debussy (1862-1918) began this trend. He
looked like a typical Bohemian painter, with his big,
flowing cravats, his wide, pale face, enormous forehead
across which a dense lock of hair fell, and soft dark eyes.

But whereas we generally think of Bohemian art as impulsive and flighty, Debussy's whole being was discipline and intensity. His life and his music were a succession of vivid experiences—small or large—into which he entered totally. When he composed, composing absorbed him. The sea absorbed him when he sat on a bench. A single flower could absorb him, a twilight cloud—or the brooding, dolorous face of a gibbon at the zoo.

With an orchestral composition called *L'Après-midi d'un Faune* (Afternoon of a Faun), Debussy marked the decisive advent of music only hinted at by the Russian composer Modest Mussorgsky (1839-1881). Rather than try to give a realistic imitation of nature, he merely wanted to communicate the impression nature made on him. He was concerned, in this work particularly, only with giving sound colours and the possibility of depicting mood in tones instead of in formal construction. In fact, in this new tone language he had created, Debussy cast off many of the traditional rules of theory.

L'Après-midi d'un Faune was so well applauded when it was first performed on December 22, 1894, that it had to be played a second time. From then on, it clearly became Debussy's most popular piece. The flute of the faun breathed new air into musical art. The use of certain other instruments—the horn and the harp—foreshadowed the manner in which the composer employed them in his later works. Thus he cleared the way for new musical styles that have left their marks upon the twentieth century, a period as turbulently revolutionary as any since the Renaissance.

Other Impressionist composers followed Debussy. They included Ottorino Respighi, Charles Griffes, and Manuel de Falla, whose music does not consistently resemble that of his colleagues, and is, for the most part, Spanish in character and highly individualistic.

It is worth taking a closer look at the Impressionists:

Ottorino Respighi (1879-1936): Italian. A diligent and studious musician. Kept in touch with contemporary developments, but really only a passing figure in music. A fine violinist and viola player. Best-known works: *The Pines of Rome* and *La Boutique Fantastique*, based on themes by Rossini.

Maurice Ravel (1875-1937): French. Short, puny and unassuming. A pupil of Fauré. Won recognition with his *Rhapsodie Espagnole* (1907). Later wrote what is considered his masterpiece—the ballet *Daphnis and Chloe*. Developed a nervous complaint while serving with the French army in First World War. Spent the last years of his life in seclusion in the countryside near Paris.

Charles Griffes (1884-1920): American. Taught music in a boys' school and composed on the side. Died at thirty-six. One of America's outstanding composers.

Manuel de Falla (1876-1946): Spanish. One of Debussy's best friends. Had bad health all his life. Rose to be Spain's greatest composer. The ballets *El Amor Brujo* and *The Three-Cornered Hat* emerged as his most popular works. Revolutionary. Left his home in Granada, Spain for Argentina in 1940 due to unhappiness over the Spanish Civil War. Lived with his sister in South America until his death.

Claude Debussy (1862-1918): French. Eldest of five children in a poor family. Never went to school. Never learned to spell correctly. Married a culturally-deprived seamstress. So poor, he had to give a piano lesson on his wedding morning to pay for wedding breakfast. Marriage failed. Well-to-do singer left husband for Debussy in 1904. Second marriage successful. One daughter, Claude-Emma. Serious operation in 1915. First World War affected him badly. Heard explosions of bombardment of Paris in 1918. Died two days later.

Perhaps the greatest significance of Impressionism is that, born in France, with French composers among its most ardent adherents, it initially represented a reaction against the German romantic music that was winning a foothold. It was also a reaction against the growing enthusiasm for the ideas of Wagner. But it soon began to lose much of its original appeal, and in its place, around 1910, there appeared a new trend in art called "Expressionism." This lasted about twenty years and was aimed at giving expression to the artist's inner experiences. In music, this led to an abstract type of composition with distorted and often discordant melodies. A new tone language had become the chief tool of composers, reproducing in music all the passionate and psychological situations of modern life—a

31

language formulated in his youth by Arnold Schoenberg, under the influence of Wagner's opera *Tristan and Isolde*.

The German composer Richard Strauss (not to be confused with the Austrian, Johann Strauss Jr.) was also considered an Expressionistic composer, though his earlier works, influenced by such revolutionaries as Liszt, Berlioz and Wagner, are strongly Romantic. Strauss emerges as one of the most important composers, developing a tone language all his own and extending himself to the very bounds of tonality. In much, he was a pioneer and he may well have been right when he said of "modern" music, ". . . the worst part about it is that I myself started the whole sorry business."

Arnold Schoenberg (1874-1951): Austrian. Naturalized American. Began composing while a poorly-paid bank clerk. Fired for erroneously entering the name of Beethoven in a bank ledger instead of a customer's. Became a musician. Had a restless and inquiring mind. Favourite composers: Bach, Mozart, Beethoven, Brahms and Mahler. Read Balzac and Shakespeare. Admired Leonardo da Vinci, Picasso and Chagall. Taught in Boston, New York and Los Angeles. A musical pioneer.

Richard Strauss (1864-1949): German. Composed at six. Works published at seven. Also a fine conductor and pianist. Master of sonic splendour. His daring orchestral effects drew critical outrage. Now considered extremely important in the progression of musical styles. Wrote his best-known work, *Don Juan*, at twenty-one. At thirty-one, he was considered the leading modernist of his age. Married. One child.

Still under the guidance of Schoenberg, Expressionism eventually developed into a type of music called "atonality" which violates most music we hear in so far as it is not related to either a major or minor key. This later spurred the introduction of a more advanced form of atonality called "twelve-tone music" or "music of the twelve-tone system," developed by Schoenberg between 1911 and 1923.

Contrary to common belief, Schoenberg did not invent twelve-tone music. This honour rightly belonged to the Viennese Joseph Mathias Hauer (1883-1959) who died broken, unknown and embittered because the world looked upon the new technique as belonging exclusively to Schoenberg, while it was *he* who was primarily concerned with its development.

Schoenberg's first experiments with the twelve-tone system were in the last number of *Five Pieces for Piano* and in the fourth movement of his *Serenade* for seven instruments and baritone, composed in 1923. The following year, he launched his first work constructed entirely on the twelve-tone system—his *Suite for Piano*. With this he opened a new horizon of sound values.

Twelve-tone music has been the subject of many books, by virtue of its complexity and revolutionary influence. Basically, it makes little and oftentimes no use of the traditional and familiar concepts of melody, harmony and tonality. It derives its name because it is based on the twelve notes of the chromatic scale instead of the eight notes of the familiar octave—Do - Re - Mi - Fa - So - La - Ti - Do. These twelve notes of the chromatic scale are easily identified by starting anywhere on the piano and playing all the white and black keys consecutively. Further, while the familiar scale recognizes half notes, twelve-tone music regards all notes of equal value, thus providing a completely different basis for variations of pitch. This results in "unusual" intervals of sound, and the composer strives earnestly to permute his twelve tones without assigning more value to one note than any other—and to avoid any semblance of a melody.

Twelve-tone music, then, is not melodious in the way we have come to look upon melody, because it abolishes the key note—Do. Schoenberg and his twelve-tone pupils, including Alban Berg and Anton Webern, believed that the new system freed them from the "tyranny of tonality" and allowed them more time to concentrate on rhythm.

Composers who have employed the twelve-tone technique include:

Alban Berg (1855-1935): Austrian. Composed more than seventy pieces before the age of seventeen. Undoubtedly a musical innovator. Besides being his pupil, he was Schoenberg's close friend. Began twelve-tone composing in 1921. Best-known work: *Wozzeck*, an opera. Died on Christmas day from blood poisoning.

Anton Webern (1883-1945): Austrian. Ph.D. from the University of Vienna at twenty-two. Held important conducting posts. Conducted the Vienna Workers'

Symphony Concerts. Lived in semi-retirement from 1918 on, devoting time to teaching and composing. Accidentally killed by gunfire during the occupation of Austria at the close of the Second World War.

Igor Stravinsky (1882-1971): American. Russian-born. Important musical figure. Son of an opera singer. Studied law. Pupil of Rimsky-Korsakov. His ballet, *The Rite of Spring,* drew severe criticism for its hardness at its first performance in 1931. Such other works as *The Firebird* and *Petrushka* were well received. Saw Russia for the last time in 1914. Later lived in Switzerland, France and the United States. Interested in the peculiarities of jazz.

Karlheinz Stockhausen (1928-   ): German. First important electronic composer. Lectured widely in the United States and Europe. Also wrote orchestral compositions.

When Stockhausen produced the very first composition with synthetic sounds in 1952, he started a tidal wave. We have been deluged with electronics ever since, in all kinds of music—including pop and oriental—ninety per cent of which sounds like water bubbling down the plughole. Stockhausen himself regards the creation of a new musical sound through electronic means as a revolutionary idea akin to the splitting of the atom. In years to come, we may well look back on what he has started, just as we now look back on those musical periods that have gone before us, and refer to it calmly as the Age of Electronics. What then?

A number of fine composers, known as the "Post-Romanticists," were working at the same time as Schoenberg, though in an entirely different manner. Four of these were Englishmen—the first important products of Britain since Henry Purcell, two hundred years before:

Frederick Delius (1862-1934): One of eleven children. Father a well-to-do wool merchant of German extraction. Trained for his father's business but rejected it in favour of composing. Began at nineteen. Persuaded his father to buy him an orange plantation in Florida. Often went to Jacksonville where Negro music was great influence. Grieg persuaded Delius' father to give his son a yearly allowance for music. By 1925 Delius was lame and blind. Died aged seventy-two.

Gustav Holst (1874-1934): Descendant of a Swedish family. Began composing early. Acquired considerable experience as a village church organist. Later joined the Carl Rosa Opera Company as a trombonist. Also became director of music at St. Paul's Girls' School, London. Friend of Ralph Vaughan Williams who helped him. Best known works: *The Planets Suite* and *The Perfect Fool*, an opera.

Ralph Vaughan Williams (1872-1958): Born into a comfortable family in Gloucestershire village. Father the rector; his mother Margaret Jane Wedgewood of Wedgewood pottery fame. Took his first piano lessons from an aunt, Miss A. Wedgewood, at five. Favourite composers: Handel, Haydn and Mozart. Later wrote operas, fine songs and powerful symphonic works. Conducted many of his own compositions. During Second World War he addressed envelopes and trundled a garbage barrow through Dorking, Surrey. Also became the chairman of a Home Office voluntary committee to advise on release of certain alien musicians interned.

Sir Edward Elgar (1857-1934): English. Father kept a music shop. Organist, pianist and bassoonist in the local orchestra. Originally set out to be a solicitor. First professional music appointment at twenty: bandmaster at a mental hospital. Lacked general encouragement. Did not begin composing seriously until his early thirties. Composed prolifically from 1900 to 1920 when his wife died. Nothing important afterwards. Best known works: *Violin Concerto, Enigma Variations* and *Pomp and Circumstance Marches*.

Other twentieth-century composers, generally thought to be more significant because they formulated new ideas and trends, were:

Serge Prokofiev (1891-1953): Russian. First piano lessons from his mother. Composed first pieces at five. Began studying composition seriously at thirteen under Rimsky-Korsakov. Earliest works considered too modern by audiences who walked out. Communist party found his music too intellectual. Told Prokofiev to "mend his ways." He did—in later works. But earlier compositions, including *Peter and The Wolf* and *The Love of Three Oranges*, are considered his finest.

Dmitri Shostakovich (1906-   ): Russian. Early instruction from his mother, a pianist. Wrote the first of twelve symphonies while a student in Leningrad. Influenced greatly by Rimsky-Korsakov, Tchaikovsky and Prokofiev. Later wrote operas, piano music and incidental music for plays and films. Decorated with the Order of Lenin by the Soviet government.

Sergei Rachmaninoff (1873-1943): Russian. Also a fine pianist. *Prelude in C Sharp Minor* made him world-famous at twenty. Friend of Tchaikovsky. Left Russia in 1917 during the Revolution. Never saw Russia again. No great sympathy for "modern" music; tended to carry Romanticism well into twentieth century. Exceptional technical ability. Died in Beverley Hills, California.

Roger Sessions (1896-   ): American. By thirteen he had written an opera. Went to Harvard at fourteen. Later went to Yale. Works difficult to perform; not often heard.

Jean Sibelius (1865-1957): Finnish. Son of an army doctor. When young formed a chamber trio with his sisters. Finnish government gave him a life pension in appreciation of his talent. Wrote *Finlandia*, a patriotic work and his most famous. Married. Five children.

Benjamin Britten (1913-   ): English. Wrote a string quartet at nine. A gifted pianist. Bachelor. Wrote many songs for his friend, the tenor Peter Pears. Fine modern opera writer. Best known for *The Young Person's Guide to the Orchestra, Albert Herring* and *Billy Budd*. Considered one of the leading composers today.

Even though these composers were contemporaries, their works bear marked individual traits rather than characteristics of an era—further documentation, perhaps, that upon the advent of the twentieth century music widened its frontiers much more drastically than ever before via orchestral technique, exploratory compositional technique, or mode of expression. Indeed, music of the twentieth century breaks all boundaries in its break for freedom, and presents the most complex picture in musical history, largely because, for the first time, virtually everything is acceptable.

Suggested Listening:

Impressionism

Debussy:	*Images for Orchestra, Afternoon of a Faun, La Mer*
Ravel:	*Daphis and Chloe, Rhapsodie Espagnole, La Valse, Boléro*

Music of the Twentieth Century

Schoenberg:	*Five Pieces for Orchestra*
Webern:	*Five Movements for String Quartet*
Williams:	*Fantasia on a Theme by Tallis, Fantasia on Greensleeves*
Stravinsky:	*Firebird Suite, Pulcinella Suite, Petrushka*
Elgar:	*Enigma Variations*

The Orchestra

(5) *its instruments, the woodwinds,
the brass section and brass bands,
the percussion instruments, the
stringed instruments, the wind
instruments, early orchestras*

Any reasonably-sized combination of instruments is considered to be an orchestra today. The symphony orchestra, which may have more than one hundred players, is the largest. It consists of stringed instruments, woodwinds, brass and percussion. A chamber orchestra may have the same instruments but is much smaller. A stringed orchestra is made up of stringed instruments alone. A theatre orchestra is usually an ensemble small enough to fit into a theatre's orchestra pit, and can be adjusted accordingly. It can also be made to include such instruments as the saxophone, not normally used in either a chamber or symphony orchestra.

Many people are confused when they hear the word "philharmonic" used to describe an orchestra. Taken from the Greek, "philharmonic" simply means "friend of music," and does not denote any particular

The celebrated Berlin Chamber Octet, one of many chamber ensembles specializing in small-scale music of the Baroque and Classical periods. Notice the type of instruments the musicians use.

kind of orchestra, choral group, or concert hall to which it is often prefixed.

The largest body of instruments in any orchestra is inevitably the family of strings, comprising violins, violas, cellos and double basses. All are played by bowing, although sometimes they are plucked, a technique known as pizzicato. Because these instruments are fragile and the sounds they make are relatively small, with the exception of the double basses, they are usually found at the front of the orchestra, nearest the audience.

The principal member of the string family is the violin. It is also the smallest instrument and, strangely enough, has not been improved upon or altered since its first appearance in the sixteenth century. The Italian Gaspero da Salo (1540-1609) is said to have made the first four-string violin. The craft was later developed at the turn of the sixteenth and seventeenth centuries by such violin-making families as the Amati, the Guarneri, and the greatest of them all, the Stradivari. The stringed instruments of Antonio Stradivari (1644-1737), a student of Andrea Amati (1520-1580), were so expertly created that they have yet to be surpassed, let alone improved upon. Andrea's sons, Francesco (1671-1743)

39

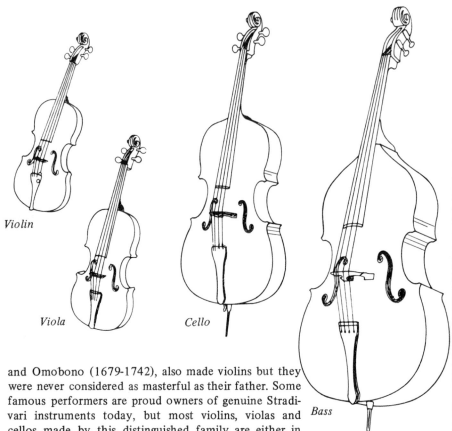

Violin

Viola

Cello

Bass

and Omobono (1679-1742), also made violins but they were never considered as masterful as their father. Some famous performers are proud owners of genuine Stradi-vari instruments today, but most violins, violas and cellos made by this distinguished family are either in museums or private collections.

The violins are nearly always seated on the left of the conductor and are divided into two sections known as first violins and second violins because they play different musical parts.

On the conductor's right, just opposite the violins, are the violas, the tenor members of the string family. The viola is another important instrument, one-seventh larger than the violin and tuned one-fifth of an octave lower. Its tone is more muted and has less brilliance and power than that of the violin, but it nevertheless has a quality of its own that has made it a favourite instru-ment of such composers as Paul Hindemith (1895-1963) and Bela Bartok (1881-1945), both of whom have written fine works especially for it.

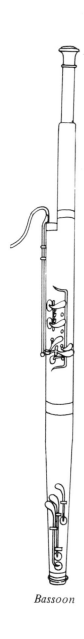

Bassoon

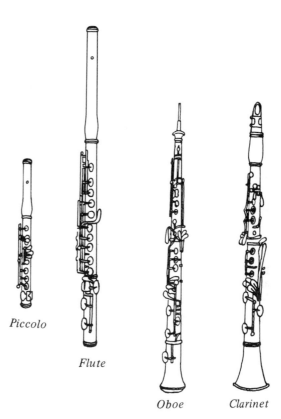

Piccolo

Flute

Oboe *Clarinet*

Just behind the violas you will usually find the cellos (or violoncellos), although these sometimes sit opposite the violins at the front of the orchestra. The cello, the baritone member of the violin family, is twice as big as the violin. It possesses a low, mellow quality that makes it much more popular as a solo instrument than the viola. Many compositions have been written especially for it, of which those by Haydn, Elgar, Dvorak and Richard Strauss emerge as among the finest.

The largest member of the stringed section is the double bass, also called a string bass, contrabass or simply, bass. Because of its size, it has the lowest sound of all the strings. Its tone is deep and heavy and its range is only two-and-a-half octaves, although some experienced double bass players have been able to extend this to three octaves. The double bass, found mostly in symphony orchestras and dance bands, has been given virtually no solo music whatsoever, and only a few works for chamber ensembles have even included it.

41

There is a part for the double bass in Schubert's string quintet, *The Trout*, however.

Jazz gains dimension by the deep, pizzicato passages it gives to the double bass. Jazz recognizes that, apart from having the lowest sound among the strings of the orchestra, the double bass also has the biggest. (This explains why it is usually found near the rear of the symphony orchestra.)

The placement of the strings varies according to the whim of the conductor or the acoustics of the concert hall. Some conductors might place their double basses near the audience, just behind the cellos. They might also interchange the violas with the second violins. It's all a matter of taste and tradition.

French Horn

In the woodwind section of the modern orchestra you may find any combination of such instruments as piccolos, flutes, oboes, English horns (often called Cor anglais), clarinets, bass-clarinets, bassoons, contra-bassoons and sometimes even a saxophone. Each consists basically of a tube housing a column of air which vibrates when the instrument is blown into. This column of air is either lengthened or shortened when the player opens or closes holes in the tube with his fingers. In so doing, he varies the pitch of the notes he plays.

The woodwind instruments can, however, be divided into two categories—those like the flute and piccolo which produce sound by vibrating solely in the flue or pipe and those like the oboe, English horn, clarinet, bass-clarinet, saxophone, bassoon and contra-bassoon which have the added help of a mouthpiece reed. The clarinet, the bass-clarinet and the saxophone have one reed; the others have what is called a double reed.

Other wind instruments *not* normally found in the orchestra are:

Flue-voiced: fife, pipe and recorder
Reed-voiced: bagpipe, bassett horn, harmonica and mouth organ

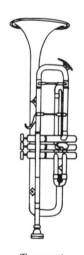

Trumpet

Like the strings, behind which they are placed in the orchestra, the pitch of the woodwind instruments is regulated by their size. The piccolo, first, and then the flute provide the highest notes, and the bassoon and the larger contra-bassoon, not found in music until this century, provide the lowest. The clarinets and oboes

42

have similar in-between ranges, as do the bass-clarinets and saxophones, but they are placed lower.

The brass section of the orchestra is capable of making the biggest noise, and contains such basic instruments as French horns, trumpets, tenor and bass trombones, and sometimes the cornet and the tuba (the biggest of the brass family). These instruments are played by being blown into directly through either a cup-shaped or funnel-shaped mouthpiece, and are so called because they are usually made of brass. Some, however, are being manufactured today in various other metals.

Some brass instruments belong almost exclusively to the brass band. They include the euphonium, the mellophone (like the French horn), the bugle, the flugelhorn, and various other types of horn generally not heard in a symphony orchestra unless a composer specifically asks for them.

One of the most famous additions to the brass family is the Sousaphone, created by the American John Philip Sousa (1854-1932) who sought a certain dimension to his band music that he felt no other instrument could give. The Sousaphone, still used today when brass bands all over the world play such well-known Sousa marches as "The Stars and Stripes Forever," "Washington Post" and "Hands Across the Sea," is a kind of tuba with a large bell which encircles the player's body. Apart from wanting a specific bass sound, Sousa designed his Sousaphone to replace the tuba which, he felt, was too difficult for a bandsman to hold while on the march.

Although Sousa's brass bands enjoyed a worldwide reputation, the tradition of playing music on the march was started some years before his birth. Indeed, the first bands consisting solely of brass instruments made their appearance in the 1830's. The first was formed by employees in an iron works organization in Blaina, Monmouthshire, Wales, in 1832. The following year, the York Waits formed a band of twenty-four men. Then, in 1835, a similar organization was begun by Ernst Klussmann, horn player in King George IV's private band and later bandmaster of the Ninth Lancers.

In those early days, brass bands served two main purposes—as aids to cavalry regiments either in battle or on parade, and as vehicles for amateur music-making. Then inception saw the birth of a tradition of band concerts and competitions which never failed to draw

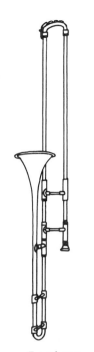

Trombone

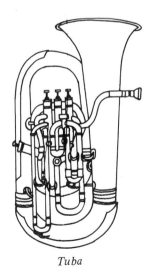

Tuba

large crowds and musicians from many parts of Europe. The earliest record of a brass band concert reaches back to 1818. Three years later, at a celebration honouring King George IV, the Besses o' th' Barn, formed in 1853, won a competition with "God Save the King" as its self-selected test piece.

Brass band concerts and competitions are still held in Europe today, particularly in Britain where, by the beginning of the twentieth century, there were as many as 20,000 such organizations, military and otherwise, vying for an assortment of prizes. Among top military bands in England are those of the Royal Air Force, The Grenadier Guards and the Royal Army Medical Corps. Perhaps Britain's most famous civilian or "works" band is that of the Black Dyke Mills, inaugurated at a group of Lancashire cotton mills in 1855.

The main difference between the civilian brass band and the military band is one of composition. Usually, the military band comprises fewer woodwind instruments than the "works" band. In recent years,

One of the finest military bands ever assembled, the Band of the Grenadier Guards plays during the changing of the guard at Buckingham Palace.

44

however, many military bands have enlarged themselves to include virtually every instrument that can be blown. These bands, in turn, are often called "symphonic bands" and are capable of performing adaptations of a wide selection of symphonic music. But whatever they are and wherever they are, most bands and orchestras draw on the final family of instruments—the percussion.

Once a pair of kettle drums was enough for a band, but now there is a whole battery of percussion instruments, not only struck, but stroked and shaken as well. These can be divided into two groups—instruments made of resonating surfaces with stretched skins and those made of wood or metal. Percussion instruments can also be further divided between those that have definite pitch (the tympani, celesta, xylophone, chimes, bells and the glockenspiel) and those that have no definite pitch (bass drums, side drums, tambourines, wood blocks, castanets, cymbals and gongs).

Three examples of works in which there is a striking use of percussion instruments are Bartok's *Music for Strings, Percussion and Celesta*, Stravinsky's *Les Noces* and Milhaud's *Concerto for Percussion and Small Orchestra*. Earlier, Beethoven used drums effectively in the thunderstorm section of his *Sixth Symphony*, the "Pastorale."

When all the instruments of an orchestra combine simultaneously, we have what is often referred to as the "giant orchestra," which encompasses the greatest possible range of tonal combinations and special effects. This was the dream of Berlioz and Wagner who, furthering the cause of Romanticism, were by no means satisfied with their contemporary orchestras. Berlioz, for instance, wanted to see an organization comprising 242 strings, sixty-two woodwinds, forty-seven brass instruments, thirty harps, thirty grand pianos, an organ, eight pairs of kettle drums, and a percussion section of forty-seven—a total of 467 members. Added to this, he wanted a choir of 360! He didn't actually compose any works for an orchestra of this magnitude, but his requirements for a religious work called *Requiem and Te Deum* do not fall far short of it.

The orchestrations of Berlioz, though, proved of enormous significance to Wagner who made the harp a permanent member of the orchestra. A characteristic feature of Wagner's orchestration is his treatment of the strings, each section being split into innumerable subdivisions. When he embarked on a four-opera cycle called *The Ring*, he demanded an orchestra of 104 persons, thus beginning the era of the giant orchestra, and finally effecting the Romanticists' dream.

Instrumentalists have played together to accompany dancers and other stage performers from very early times. The first orchestras approaching the modern concept, however, appeared during the late Renaissance. These consisted chiefly of wind instruments. Not until the late seventeenth century did strings begin to be used widely. That was when J.S. Bach gave them prominence. He was certainly one of the first composers to incorporate the masterpieces of Stradivari, Guarneri and Amati into the orchestra and, in so doing, helped force the virtual retirement of an even earlier family of strings—the viols. Viols had six strings, instead of the four found on the Stradivari instruments, and came only in three sizes as opposed to the four in today's family of strings—treble, tenor and bass.

Most of the six-string viols lost their popularity quickly when the four-string violins and violas (then considered head of the string family) appeared. Two, however, have partially survived. They are the fifteenth-century viola da gamba which not only competed with the cello, but actually overshadowed it until well into the eighteenth century, and the seventeenth-century viola d'amore. Both these instruments are sometimes resurrected today to play music of their era, though music has been written especially for the viola d'amore within the past hundred years—by Puccini (1858-1924), Hindemith (1895-   ), and Richard Strauss.

Other stringed instruments were in use long before violins. Fingerboard contraptions, forerunners to the guitar and banjo, were in use among the earliest civilized people. The Western Asians, for instance, plucked the single string of the bow with which they hunted, using their mouths as resonators. These later developed into various noise-makers like the spade-shaped fiddles and pear-shaped liras of the eleventh century. By the fourteenth century, the guitar was born. The first guitar was not much different from the present-day instrument, except that it had four strings instead of six. The two extra strings were not added until the eighteenth century when Berlioz and Paganini took up the guitar as a virtuoso instrument.

The forefather of the banjo was the mandoline, a fifteenth-century instrument of the Orient. So far as we know, the first banjo was created by the jazz-making Africans somewhere around the eleventh century, but no one is certain about this. The Russians adapted it during the last century, and it became the balalaika.

The birth of the harp dates from 2000 B.C. Many of the earliest instruments resembled hunting bows, with as many as eight strings. By about 1500 B.C., however, a more sophisticated harp was in use, one that has been traced back to the Assyrians. Lyres were commonplace then, in an assortment of designs, and were developed by the thirteenth century into various types of hand-harps. These were called psalteries, Irish harps, Tromba marinas, and hurdy-gurdies, and they cleared the way for the forerunners of the piano around the fourteenth century.

Percussion instruments seem to have preceded all others, mainly because they were easier to make and easier to play. More than 3,000 years ago the Egyptians had no mean assortment of them. There were bells, various kinds of drum, and an object called a "sistrum" which was nothing more than a series of rings strung in rows inside a frame. Like the tambourine, also used by the early Egyptians, this instrument was shaken to provide a conglomeration of small, high-pitched ringing sounds. Castanets were invented, too, and about a thousand years later, the Chinese produced musical sounds with chimes made from thin slabs of stone. The bigger the slab, the deeper the sound, the Chinese discovered, and from this invention the xylophone probably sprang.

The wind instruments have been traced to prehistoric times when men distorted their voices with a piece of hollow wood—to frighten away evil spirits. Horn-like instruments made from the tusks of various prehistoric animals were also used. Modulated through the centuries, they have given us both the brass and woodwinds sections of the modern orchestra.

But the first signs of relatively sophisticated wind instruments as we know them today were the trombone, which appeared about 1500, and the trumpet and the post horn, which date from around 1600. Two hundred years later, the trombone was larger and less crude, and the trumpet and horn were given finger valves. Apart from these changes, these instruments have remained basically the same since their first appearance.

The reeded instruments of the orchestra were developed by the early Greeks and Romans. Men found that by blowing through a hollow reed found by the

47

waterside, they could produce a high-pitched, penetrative sound that could be heard over great distances. The Arabians later introduced to Europe an early conception of a Scottish bagpipe (also reeded), and by the 1400's an instrument called a "bombard" had been developed for use in early wind ensembles.

By the early 1600's, the bombard was displaced by the bassoon, and around 1650 the oboe and the clarinet (first made by Denner in Nuremburg in 1609) appeared. The first oboe d'amore (which had a globe-shaped bell at the bottom and produced a sound lower than the ordinary oboe) was made in 1720, and appeared in public shortly afterwards.

The recorder, developed in ancient Persia and used with the bombard in the wind orchestras of the Renaissance, fell out of use in 1750. It was eventually replaced by the basset horn, from which is derived the modern saxophone, invented in 1840 by the Belgian, Adolphe Sax.

Although the modern conception of an orchestra began during the late Renaissance, the first organization of musicians known to have played together regularly was Les Vingt-quatre Violons du Roi. Under the direction of the Italian composer Jean-Baptiste Lully (1632-1687), they played before the King at the French court.

Early evidence of an orchestra of mixed instruments, however, is best illustrated by the requirements of Monteverdi (1567-1648). For his opera *Orpheus* in 1607 he used:

Strings	*Wind instruments*
10 violins	4 trombones
3 viola da gamba	4 trumpets
2 violino piccolo	3 small organs
2 double basses	2 cornets
2 harpsichords	1 flute
2 large lutes	
1 harp	

In time, the strings became divided into four sections—first violins, second violins, violas, and cellos and double basses together. Jean-Phillipe Rameau (1683-1764) later developed Bach's conception of an orchestra with strings and woodwinds. The next important step came around 1750 (the year of Bach's death) by the Mannheimers, generally regarded as the founders of the symphony orchestra as we have come to know it today. They used:

Wind instruments	Strings
2 flutes	first violins
2 oboes	second violins
2 bassoons	violas
2 horns	cellos
2 trumpets	double basses
Percussion	
2 kettle-drums	

In the second half of the 1700's, two clarinets were added to form the usual orchestra for which Haydn (1732-1809) and Mozart (1756-1791) usually wrote. Beethoven (1770-1827) saw the horns increased from two to four and the occasional addition of trombones. He was also the first composer to separate the cellos from the double basses, giving the strings a fifth section. It was the orchestra as Beethoven conceived it that was used to play the works of Rossini, Schumann, Verdi, Liszt, Brahms, Grieg, Bizet, Dvorak, Franck and Sibelius. It had obviously been widely accepted.

Suggested Listening:

Britten:	*Young Person's Guide to the Orchestra*
Bartok:	*Music for Strings, Percussion and Céleste*
Stravinsky:	*Les Noces, Octet for Wind Instruments*
Milhaud:	*Concerto for Percussion and Small Orchestra*

The conductor and his orchestra

(6) *the role of the conductor, his technique, rehearsals, famous conductors, the conductor through the ages, conductor-composers*

Even though each player might have learned his part well and acquired a flawless sense of ensemble, the finest orchestra in the world would only be a shadow of itself without a conductor. Experiments in this direction were carried out more than twenty years ago when audiences in the United States, the Soviet Union and Hungary were invited especially to hear orchestras perform without conductors, but the results were generally considered to have been without much artistic merit. Because they comprised superb musicians, the orchestras played well, technically. But many of the basic elements of good performance—elements we often take for granted—were missing. Variations in pace and volume were not sufficiently contrasted, and this meant that the music was not only dull, but without depth of interpretation. The critics unanimously felt that the orchestra without a conductor merely offered a mechanical rendition. It needed someone to lead it—someone to inject dynamics, draw out tonal colours, and generally stamp the performance with a mark of individuality.

This, then, in simple terms, is the role of the conductor. Relatively few musicians succeed in becoming conductors, partly because there are relatively few orchestras, and partly because conducting is a highly specialized art. Ask the average concert-goer what he knows about it and you will hear some strange theories. On the one hand, people tend to think that the conductor is either the sole creator of the music or the orchestrator. On the other hand, they think that he is merely a part of tradition—a superfluous ornament or clown in black tails who has been sent before the audience to entertain with a repertoire of stock gestures and gymnastics. Some amateur conductors, of course, slip comfortably into this category. They might just as well not be there, for all the good they do. But when we talk of professional orchestras, this is by no means the case.

It is also generally accepted by the public that the conductor's first obligation to his players is to give them a tempo. It would be wrong, however, to think that this was the most significant part of his job. Equally, it would be incorrect to suggest that the conductor only feels the music in his hands. On the contrary, he must feel it in his entire body. Basically, his first obligation is to acquaint himself thoroughly with the composer's score and, ostensibly, feel it from his toes to his scalp. His musical ideas and feelings at that time manifest themselves in the gestures seen by the audience. Under different emotional circumstances and on other occasions, the conductor will have different musical ideas, and it is these that account for his never interpreting a work in exactly the same way twice.

A saying not uncommon among conductors is, "I can even lead an orchestra with my eyebrows." If we accept that a conductor feels music right to his scalp, this may well be possible. But it is generally felt that more movement than that is required to conduct music adequately. The question has prompted some controversy. The young conductors today invariably tend to be athletic, whereas older ones tend to feel that only a slight movement of the baton is required to bring an orchestra to life. The Hungarian-born Fritz Reiner (1888-1963), a former musical director of the Chicago Symphony and certainly one of the finest conductors of the century, moved very little. A story goes that while

51

rehearsing Dvorak's *New World Symphony*, a double-bass player complained, "Doctor Reiner, I cannot see your beat."

"Get a telescope," snapped Reiner.

The double-bass player did. He arrived for the following day's rehearsal early and set up the telescope so that he could saw at his instrument freely yet enjoy a magnificent view of Reiner's minuscule movements. But his glory lasted just ten minutes. It ended abruptly when Reiner saw the telescope pointing at him like an accusing finger, produced a tiny piece of paper and a pencil from his pocket, and wrote a quick note to the double-bass player who saw it through his telescope.

The note said, "You're fired!"

With his movements, the conductor is expected to breathe life, urgency and enthusiasm into his players and hope that they, in turn, respond by reflecting these qualities in their playing. In performance, he must also concern himself with the balance of sound and acoustics. But he must never lose sight of one major factor—that he is there at the service of the composer. These aspects are especially important if the conductor and his orchestra are performing a standard work which nearly everyone knows. In new works, most members of the audience will not be able to make comparisons. Nevertheless, the conductor should still concern himself with the climaxes, rhythms, paces and colours of sound for which the composer originally asked.

The conductor generally employs a baton to express his musical ideas, though he may sometimes choose to use only his hands. I once saw Erich Leinsdorf, musical director of the Boston Symphony, conduct a complete performance of a Beethoven symphony without a baton.

A baton, however, is considered a definite aid to a conductor, and in the hands of an expert it can be made to express a wide range of musical subtleties. At one moment the conductor might have his baton loosely poised and, by using wrist motions, use only its tip to depict the smoothness and slowness of an *adagio*. At the next, he might grip his baton like a hammer and thrash out large, crisp, round staccatos. The method he chooses to elicit these effects is always his own choice, and to triumph artistically he must have created a reservoir of orchestral resources from which he can draw at any given moment—either in the informal atmosphere of the rehearsal room or before the audience.

That the conductor must be a talented and fine musician himself goes without saying. He must not only know his theory and the rudiments of music well, but comprehend the capabilities of every instrument and every player in his ensemble so that he never asks for the impossible. He should clearly be the most solid musician in the organization, always able to answer questions on theoretical points in the score and to discuss matters of interpretation at any given moment.

The French conductor Pierre Boulez tells us something about the intellectual aspect of his work and the need for analysis when he says, "I've learned a lot about composing from conducting, and composing helps me conduct. I can see the interior of a composition. Mostly, it is the exterior, the trappings, which seduce people. I want to provoke not just an emotional, but an intellectual response to the structure behind the sound."

The German conductor Erich Leinsdorf is shown conducting an orchestra of young musicians during a visit to Canada.

While the theory of music and the technique of conducting can, and must be, thoroughly learned, neither would be of much use without inborn artistic qualities. Here the difference between the conductor's being outstanding or merely competent depends on the combination of the technical aspect of his work plus that which he is expected to "feel" to the depth of his soul. He must have a passion for his music so that he can impart it to the members of the orchestra.

There is yet another quality imperative for a conductor: he must have a strong sense of leadership. However musical he might be, members of an orchestra would soon lose both respect and faith in a man who lacked the ability to maintain discipline.

It goes without saying, that while the players must have an unerring sense of ensemble, the conductor must have an unerring ear for tempo. It is also true, however, that only a bad conductor stands before an orchestra for the sole purpose of mapping out a beat.

The art of conducting is both individual and controversial. Usually a conductor sets his beat with the baton, and uses his free hand to ensure that various instruments or sets of instruments make accurate entrances. There are times, though, when the pulse or beat of the music is so well set that he can use both hands to help his players into *crescendos* (when the music gets louder), *diminuendos* (when the music gets softer) and *rallantandos* (when the music gets gradually slower, usually at the end of a work). He can also help them to master the phrasing, a vitally important part of music.

53

Phrases are a chain of notes forming a distinct unit of melody. The notes may be long or short, but whatever their length, they have to comprise a phrase that has both a firm beginning and a clean ending—rather like a sentence in good writing. The conductor must also ensure that his musicians understand the meaning behind each phrase. If that meaning is to be transmitted to the audience, phrases must be separated by a slight and natural pause, or "breathing" space. More important, though, the conductor must ensure that each phrase remains part of the music as a whole and that the composition, however long or short it may be, is successful in its entirety and not merely in isolated patches.

The conductor's major difficulty on the technical side is seeing that, to avoid raggedness, his musicians do everything together. This part of his job is not an easy one. A typical symphony orchestra employs about one hundred instruments—and sometimes more—distributed as follows:

Strings	Woodwinds
18 first violins	3 flutes
16 second violins	1 piccolo
12 violas	3 oboes
10 cellos	1 English horn
8 double basses	3 clarinets
2 harps	1 bass clarinet
	3 bassoons
	1 double bassoon

Brass	Percussion
6 French horns	4 timpani
4 trumpets	1 glockenspiel
4 trombones	tenor drums
1 tuba	bass drum
	xylophone

There is a distinct advantage in going to a concert rather than hearing a performance on records—if only to see the conductor. In the concert hall you can watch his motions and gestures and relate these to the sounds that are emitted from the orchestra. Sometimes you can anticipate the textures of sounds the conductor wants to draw and after a while you should be able to decide for yourself whether he is leading his orchestra with conviction, or whether his orchestra is leading *him*—in which case he has failed.

Most of the conductor's work is done long before he and his orchestra ever see the audience. If he happens to be the musical director of an organization (Eugene Ormandy is musical director of the Philadelphia Orchestra, for instance), he will have the added job of selecting his musicians and generally administrating the artistic side of the organization. He chooses his musicians at auditions held once every year. The administrative side of his work also finds him selecting concert tours and solo artists to perform with his orchestra during the season. He is also involved in a host of other details about which few people ever hear. While the musical director of a symphony orchestra invariably has a staff to assist him, he is usually the main decision-maker. Certainly he has the final say in such matters as repertoire and the amount of rehearsals needed for each concert.

Rehearsals can be long and tedious, with the conductor taking his orchestra repeatedly over the same short passages in the score until he is artistically satisfied with what has been produced. His musicians work diligently on all aspects of the score, both at home and in the rehearsal room—just as an actor works diligently on his lines before the performance of a play.

It would not be outrageous, in fact, to compare the conductor of a musical organization with the theatre director. Both are concerned with interpretation, pace, variations of volume and entertaining an audience. Both must be primarily concerned with performing a work faithfully, so that it corresponds with how the composer or writer would have wanted to hear it.

Another important facet of the performance with which the conductor is concerned in rehearsal is that of shading and balance. He may want a bigger sound from the brass or woodwinds in one section, and may want the strings to ride above everything else in another. When he gets into the concert hall, though, he may find that because of the acoustics he must adjust his shading and balance all over again. He usually does this with his left hand, leaving his right hand free to guide the entire organization up to the inevitable climaxes that make music, like literature, exciting. But it takes a great deal of experience to achieve all this.

You will understand, then, that if ever you went backstage to visit the conductor during a concert, you would invariably find him sitting in his dressing room studying the score of the next work on the programme.

55

It is not a question of insecurity or indecision. It is necessary for him to begin to "feel" the power of the music before he reaches the podium, and have the tempos firmly set in his mind. Tempo, of course, is of utmost importance. Played too slowly, music can be dull; played too quickly, it can lose the composer's initial meaning.

Tempo, incidentally, is an Italian word meaning "time." In music, it refers to the rate of speed at which the music is to be performed, as stipulated by the composer on his score.

Here are some common tempo indications:

Largo:	very slow and broad
Lento:	slow
Adagio:	slow, but not quite as slow as lento
Andante:	at a walking pace
Moderato:	moderate speed
Allegretto:	moderately fast
Allegro:	quite fast
Presto:	very fast
Prestissimo:	extremely fast

Many of these are undeniably a matter of opinion. What is very fast to me may be extremely fast to you. But this is where the conductor has to combine his good judgement with the exuberance he feels as he stands before his orchestra. He must also consider that if he takes a particular section too quickly, some of his musicians may have difficulty negotiating it. For example, while the strings and woodwinds may be playing slowly, the brass may have appreciably faster work.

It is worth talking more about the sense of ensemble. This is imperative in a symphony orchestra because, ideally, all musicians, though playing their own particular parts, listen to the others, too. In pop music, it is usually more essential for each player or singer to be individualistic during a performance. In symphonic music, however, this kind of individuality is, for the most part, discouraged. Only when a player is given a solo can he afford to be an individual. At other times, he is sitting in the orchestra at the sole service of the music and not for his own acclamation. If anyone seeks acclamation, it is the conductor who untiringly and oftentimes energetically shapes orchestral sounds so they correspond with his own image of how the composer wanted them.

There has always been some controversy as to how much the conductor should inflict his own personality upon the music. The Russian-American Serge Koussevitsky (1874-1951), for instance, maintained that a conductor should have freedom to choose tempo, interpretation and shading for himself, thus imposing his own personality on the performance. But the German conductor Felix Weingartner (1863-1942) felt the exact opposite. One of the most outstanding musical interpreters of his day, he felt the entire job of the conductor was to follow the composer's intentions closely—to be his humble servant and interpreter.

Arturo Toscanini (1867-1957) felt this way, too. Unquestionably, this made him one of the foremost conductors of the twentieth century. It is unfortunate that he did not live into the stereophonic era of recording and that we are thus unable to reproduce the true power, quality, sonic range and colour of his orchestra. The subtleties are still there, though, and they more than document Toscanini's musical genius, which men are still striving to describe. In his book *The Toscanini Legacy* (published by Dover Publications Inc. in 1969), Spike Hughes says: "That Toscanini will prove to be one of the immortals of music I think there is little doubt. He became a legend in his lifetime; his legacy of recordings at least will substantiate most of what was said in praise of him. It is up to us now to see that what we have inherited from him is recognized and preserved as a tremendous manifestation of a spirit of passionate devotion to music and untiring pursuit of perfection in its execution which must not be lost to posterity. . . . There will never be another Arturo Toscanini."

Toscanini, volatile and tempestuous, was perhaps best known for his interpretations of the Italian opera. Sought after by the world's major opera houses, he conducted at virtually all of them. He was also known for his conducting of the works of Respighi, whom he knew well and understood. His strength lay in his supreme ability to feel a wide range of emotions and to induce his musicians to feel them too. Hence a musical climax under Toscanini's baton was truly a climax and, though he was considered an obsessive disciplinarian and rarely ever revealed a sense of humour, he was able to

Arturo Toscanini one of the foremost conductors of the twentieth century, conducted with precision and exuberance. He was an obsessive disciplinarian, and performed virtually everything, from Italian, German and French operas to symphonies and orchestral show-pieces, from memory so he could keep his eyes firmly on the musicians.

57

Some famous conductors. Clockwise from top left:
Eugene Ormandy and pianist Rudolf Serkin, Herbert von Karajan,
Leonard Bernstein, Arturo Toscanani.

Again reading clockwise from top left: Seiji Ozawa, Sir John Barbirolli, Pierre Monteux, Fritz Reiner, Yehudi Menuhin. In the middle: Serge Koussevitzky.

extract the humour from his music in great abundance. Listen to his performances of that great fund of melody Rossini bequeathed to the world (still available on recordings) and you will see what I mean.

A famous rumour connected with Toscanini says that he never conducted from a score because he was short-sighted. But artists who worked with him tend to feel that he may have said this at some time—out of modesty. In fact, he never used the score in performance because he did not need one. He had the rare ability to conduct from it twice in rehearsal, and then know the music completely by heart thereafter, never to forget it. A score to Toscanini was more of a hindrance than a help; he preferred to keep his eyes and ears on the orchestra.

Apart from Toscanini, other important conductors include:

Hans von Bulow (1830-1894): German. Also a pianist but considered a cold performer. As a conductor, eccentric and theatrical. Established conducting as a complex and important art. Taught Richard Strauss. Remarkable memory. Conducted without a score. Considered the best interpreter of Beethoven. Married Liszt's daughter. Later surrendered her to Wagner, his friend.

Hans Richter (1843-1916): Hungarian. Studied with Wagner. Honoured by city of Vienna for outstanding and important conducting. Played piano and French horn.

Carl Muck (1859-1940): German. Stern and rigid. Also a concert pianist. One of the earliest conductors of the Boston Symphony. Accused of anti-American activity in 1918. Imprisoned for fourteen months in Georgia and deported. Later conducted in all major cities.

Sir Thomas Beecham (1879-1961): English. Witty. Married twice. Angry with audiences that coughed or applauded too soon. Champion of Mozart, Delius, Stravinsky, Richard Strauss and Berlioz. Also a good opera conductor. Founded two fine orchestras: the Royal Philharmonic and the London Philharmonic. Father a tycoon and manufacturer of Beecham's Liver Pills.

Guido Cantelli (1920-1956): Italian. Protégé of

Sir Thomas Beecham enjoyed a long, varied and colourful career as an international conductor of the world's finest orchestras. Some of his recordings are still available and are cherished by collectors.

Toscanini. Youthful and vigorous. Killed in air crash after having conducted throughout the world.

Wilhelm Furtwaengler (1886-1954): German. Particularly temperamental. Nominated to succeed Toscanini as conductor of the New York Philharmonic in 1936. Cancelled the engagement due to controversy among subscribers as to his political and racial sympathies. Lavished with musical honours by German government. Some, however, chastised him for being "pro-Russian."

Bruno Walter (1876-1962): German. Conducted in the great German tradition. Encouraged by Mahler. Resigned as musical director of the Berlin Philharmonic in 1933, following the election of the National Socialist government. Also composed chamber works and songs.

Ernest Ansermet (1883-1969): Swiss. Mathematician, writer and lecturer. Founder of L'Orchestre de la Suisse Romande. Friend of Stravinsky, many of whose works he premiered.

The advancement of recordings presents us today with a wide choice of talented conductors—far too many, in fact, to list in a book. Like their predecessors, these conductors have their weaknesses, their strengths and their preferences. They are also trying to bring to music a new dimension by being faithful to the composer, by using the recording medium to its fullest potential in the presentation of full-blooded musical sounds (something many of the equally fine and earlier conductors were not able to do), and by enhancing their work with a stamp of individuality. Names like Otto Klemperer, Herbert von Karajan, Colin Davies, Georg Solti, Leonard Bernstein and Eugene Ormandy are familiar to many music-lovers. As music evolves, it is more than likely that each will be listed as an important contributor to an art which, in its quest for freedom, is constantly widening its boundaries. Conversely, conductors forgotten or ignored by the recording companies will remain virtually unknown.

The conductor as we know him today is a relatively modern addition to the orchestra and his position through the ages has changed several times. The first time he faced the orchestra with his back to the audience was at the opening of Wagner's Festival Theatre in

Bayreuth in 1876. Until then he was usually found in the middle of the orchestra and used either his hands or a roll of music.

According to paintings of the time, musical groups have been directed in both rehearsal and performance since about the fifteenth century. But beyond this little is known except that the "conductor" then was little more than a time-beater. Certainly some kind of conductor was needed, because music in those days was not set down as clearly as it is today, with bars and instructional notations, and someone had to be there to infuse some kind of uniformity.

By the seventeenth century, the conductor of the orchestra was sitting among his players with a stick about two yards long. He marked out the time by striking the stick heavily against the floor, but only in rehearsal. A famous musical story says that the French composer Jean-Baptiste Lully hit his big toe while conducting a cantata in 1687. Later that year he was dead from blood poisoning caused by the blow.

Conducting with the role of music, however, remained. It did not go out of fashion until early last century. As late as 1822, a member of a church audience in Italy complained that when the conductor struck his music stand with his roll of music, it sounded like the crack of a whip.

Beethoven was a busy conductor. He also preferred to sit in the middle of his players, but he chose to indicate his tempo on a harpsichord with one hand, keeping the other free to "shade" the music. He later became one of the first men to use a baton, though this technique was first introduced by Weber at a concert in 1817. Mendelssohn also used a baton—at Leipzig in 1835.

In those days, batons were made exclusively of wood. They are still available in wood today, but because most conductors prefer them of a more durable substance, they have been manufactured in plastic, bone and, more recently, in fibreglass. Some of the best batons have cork non-slip handles and are made strongly enough to withstand the sharp blow of the angry conductor on his music stand.

The conductor is the only person associated with an orchestra who can afford the luxury of temperament, and many have taken advantage of this. Beethoven was said to have been exceptionally temperamental, especially when deafness was creeping upon him. Once,

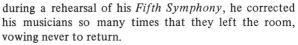

Gustav Mahler was one of the few composers able to conduct his own works. Some musicologists claim that he was a better conductor than composer, though this is open for dispute. Certainly his compositions are now enjoying wide recognition.

during a rehearsal of his *Fifth Symphony*, he corrected his musicians so many times that they left the room, vowing never to return.

Some of the best composers have been completely incapable of performing their own works in the spirit in which they were intended. Under Tchaikovsky's direction, his *Pathétique Symphony* was a miserable failure. Under the great Hungarian conductor Arthur Nikish (1855-1922), however, it met with enormous enthusiasm. On the other hand, there have been composers, like Richard Strauss and Mahler, who were outstanding conductors.

Gustav Mahler (1860-1911): Austrian. Second of twelve children. Jewish. One of the finest conductors of his day. Tyrannical and lacking in understanding for people in pursuit of his artistic ideals. Lots of enemies, forcing him to leave Vienna. Turned to conducting when his early compositions failed. Fine opera conductor. Assignments across Europe. Accepted appointment with the Metropolitan Opera, New York, in 1907. Short of money, so conducted the New York Philharmonic simultaneously. Work proved too much. Collapsed during a Philharmonic concert (his forty-seventh in three seasons) and died later in Vienna. Buried in silent reverence. Not a word spoken at the funeral, nor a note of music sung or played—Mahler's last wish. Best works: nine symphonies and a collection of fine songs.

The piano

(7) *its antecedents, its development,*
its improvement, the modern piano,
great pianist-composers·

The piano has been the standard keyboard instrument of
the civilized world since the early eighteenth century.
Until then, the harpsichord and its variants, the virginal,
clavichord and the spinet, were in popular use—but only
in fine homes, a position they had held since the time of
Queen Elizabeth I.

Virginal: A keyboard instrument popular in the sixteenth and seventeenth centuries, especially in England.
It resembled the harpsichord in that its strings were
plucked, but it was smaller and had a different shape—
usually oblong, with the keyboard running along one of
the long sides. Some virginals, however, were wing-
shaped. Important English composers of music for the
virginal were William Byrd, John Bull and Orlando
Gibbons. *The Fitzwilliam Virginal Book*, dating from
about 1620, contains 297 pieces for the virginal.

Spinet: A type of harpsichord with one keyboard, popular from about 1650 to 1800, especially in England. It was also wing-shaped and equipped with a device which plucked the strings as the keys were pressed.

Clavichord: A keyboard instrument popular in the sixteenth, seventeenth and eighteenth centuries. When a pivoted key was pressed down, a small T-shaped piece of brass (called a tangent) pressed against a brass string. The clavichord's tone is soft and delicate, making it ideal for small rooms, broadcasting and recording, but unsuitable for the concert hall. Both J.S. Bach and his son, C.P.E. Bach, wrote prolifically for the clavichord.

In the harpsichord, as in the virginals and the spinet, small picks of quill or leather were attached to mechanical fingers, or jacks. When set in motion by the keys, these rose and plucked the strings in passing. At its best, the harpsichord had a clear and brilliant tone, but it lacked the capacity for dynamic nuances and true *crescendos* and *diminuendos*. By the use of stops or pedals controlling sympathetic resonances, it could produce various timbres and fixed levels of volume, but by the nature of its action it was incapable of the flexible, intermediate shadings that gave the clavichord its special charm. No matter how ingenious the mechanism, the player lacked truly direct expressive control, for finger touch could have little effect on the tone.

Three craftsmen, however, were working independently, and probably unaware of each other, in three countries to invent a more versatile instrument. They were Marius in France, about whom little is known, Christoph Schroeter (1699-1782) in Germany, and Bartolomeo Cristofori (1665-1731) in Italy.

Since Cristofori's piano appeared first, by only a few years, he is generally credited with its invention. But there is evidence that the foundations of the piano as we know it today were laid some years before by a German violinist and dancing master with the unusual name of Pantaleon Hebenstreit. Although he was a chamber musician in the Saxon Court and an excellent violinist, Hebenstreit's favourite instrument was the dulcimer (which can be traced back to 1400), upon which he had become proficient as a boy.

Dulcimer: An instrument popular in the Middle Ages. Consisting of a number of strings of varying lengths and

65

thicknesses stretched across a shallow wooden box, it looked rather like a zither, but was played by striking the keys with hammers. Originally an Eastern instrument adopted by the folk musicians of Hungary and Rumania, the dulcimer was, at first, a rude instrument that has survived in Central and Eastern Europe as the gypsy's czimbalon. It is still used today in some folk music, and is usually plucked.

Not content with the simple form of the dulcimer as he found it, Hebenstreit greatly increased its size and added a second soundboard. He also gave it two sets of strings—one of brass and one of gut. The dulcimer now had 185 strings, strung in such a way that it could be played in all major and minor keys. Hebenstreit still played the instrument, however, in the way it had been played for many years before him—with a pair of leather-covered hammers, one in each hand.

Hebenstreit eventually became a virtuoso on this instrument and gave concert tours all over Europe, exciting great interest wherever he performed. In 1705, he played before Louis XIV who honoured him by giving the name "Pantaleon" to the improved dulcimer. The same year, and perhaps on the same concert tour, Hebenstreit performed at the Ufizzi Palace in Florence for Prince Ferdinand de Medici. Cristofori was in the audience, too, and was amazed how Hebenstreit could produce from his instrument a "whisper and a roar." It was then that he visualized how much more effective the dulcimer would be if it were linked to a keyboard instead of having its strings struck by the hand-held hammers. The idea possessed him, and within four years he exhibited to Prince Ferdinand an instrument with a keyboard and hammers for each string, called a "clavicembalo." Not only did it outmode Hebenstreit's dulcimer, but it replaced the harpsichord with its plucking quills. It also had the supreme ability to play both loudly and softly—"piano" and "forte"—from which the modern pianoforte, or piano, derives its full name.

Cristofori had first met Prince Ferdinand in Padua, his birthplace, when he was twenty-two. The prince, an able harpsichordist and mathematician interested in the mechanics of musical instruments, was visiting the town when he first heard of the young Cristofori's skill. He persuaded him to leave Padua and enter his service in Florence, where he was put in charge of the prince's splendid collection of eighty-four keyboard instruments, most of them Belgian, French and Italian. In Florence Cristofori was given a workshop, and Prince Ferdinand suggested certain improvements to keyboard instruments which Cristofori duly implemented.

After he had devised a system by which the hammers struck the strings when keys were pressed, Cristofori was faced with new problems. The strings he was using were taken from the harpsichord, and were too low in tension to give good tone. Heavier strings and greater tension were needed, and this, in turn, necessitated a stronger supporting structure. Having devised this, Cristofori then invented a system which controlled the hammers so that they sprang back into position after striking the strings.

While Cristofori's piano was being developed, the harpsichord was in a continual state of improvement and elaboration. It attained its greatest refinement at the end of the eighteenth century when it was about to yield, in popularity, to the piano. The specialization of its manufacture foreshadowed the modern piano industry, and the big harpsichords made in London at the end of the eighteenth century had the look of grand pianos in their massive appearance—unornamented and severe. Cristofori never lived to see all this. He died at sixty-six, unaware that later piano makers were to give his instrument pedals and change the size and shape of the hammer heads. The chances are, though, that Hebenstreit, the man who gave Cristofori his idea, lived to see part of the development. He outlived Cristofori and was about ninety years old when he died in 1750.

Two Cristofori pianos are known to exist today. One, dated 1720, is in the Metropolitan Museum in New York. The other, dated 1726, is in a museum in Leipzig, Germany. A harpsichord with three keyboards made by Cristofori in 1702, and bearing the coat of arms of Prince Ferdinand de Medici, belongs to the University of Michigan.

It was not until the nineteenth century that the piano really began to realize its full potentialities. With greater sonority came greater range and greater flexibility of action, and with these came greater acceptance by composers, amateur musicians and audiences. The first composer to write music designed exclusively for the piano was Muzio Clementi, whose first three sonatas for the instrument were published in 1773. Both C.P.E. and Johann Christian Bach were also instrumental in developing work for the new piano. For some time—through the early years of Beethoven—publishers brought out keyboard works styled equally "for harpsichord or piano."

Almost from the start, piano makers tried to improve the power of the instrument, to make it more expressive, and to explore its capacity for a wide dynamic range. For a louder sound they needed heavier strings, held under greater tension. These, in turn, required a heavier frame, so that the case would not collapse when the strings were tightened up to pitch.

The initial fragility of the piano has been colourfully recorded by Anton Reicha, a Czech composer and a friend of the young Beethoven, who recounted an experience that must have been paralleled many times during those early years. "One day Beethoven played at court a concerto of Mozart's, and he asked me to turn the pages for him," Reicha said. "At every moment the strings of the instrument kept snapping and jumping into the air, while the hammers got entangled in the broken strings. Beethoven, wishing to finish the piece at all cost, begged me to disengage the hammers and remove the broken strings whenever he paused in playing. My job was harder than his, for I had constantly to jump to the right, to the left, to run around the piano to get at all the troubles."

If this happened during a Mozart concerto, imagine the havoc worked by a Beethoven sonata. In 1824, Beethoven received a visit from a London harp maker, Johann Stumpff, and complained to him that on the available pianos "one can play nothing with force and effect." He showed his visitor the instrument he had received from Broadwood, whose pianos were among the sturdiest made. "What a spectacle," wrote Stumpff. "There was no sound left in the treble, and broken strings were mixed up like a thorn bush after a gale."

In 1825, an American craftsman, Alpheus Babcock of Boston, was granted a patent on a complete iron frame, cast in one piece, uniting the hitch-pin plate, which holds the strings at the rear of a grand piano, with the tuning-pin block, a laminated wooden plank in which the tuning-pins are inserted. This far-reaching improvement was not adopted by all piano makers at a single stroke, although it eventually became standard throughout the industry and is still used today. From the point of view of manufacturing stability, there was no doubt of the superiority of a single metal frame, especially those that would solve the problems of high strung tension and compensation (the need for the instrument to resist changes of temperature and humidity).

In 1821, only four years before Babcock was given his patent on the cast-iron frame, Sébastien Erard perfected the so-called double escapement mechanism that he had first patented a dozen years earlier. The suppleness and sensitivity of the modern piano action is due largely to this invention.

The modern piano has a complicated mechanism. The standard instrument has eighty-eight keys. When pressed, each causes a string to be struck in such a way that vibrations are set up. Actually, each "string" consists of one, two or sometimes three strings—one heavy string for each of the lowest tones, three strings for each tone in the centre register, and two strings for each of the higher tones. When a key is pressed, a small felt-covered piece of wood called a damper is lifted from the string, allowing the string to vibrate. When the damper pedal ("loud" pedal) is pressed, all of the dampers are raised. A flat sheet of wood called a sounding board, lying under the strings on the grand piano, and behind the strings on an upright piano, has a lot to do with the tone of the instrument. The larger the piano, the larger the sounding board—and the longer the strings. Consequently, a nine-foot concert grand piano is capable of a much larger and richer tone than a small upright.

The "soft" pedal, on the left, softens the tone by shifting the action so the hammers strike fewer strings. Some pianos have a third pedal, between the "loud" pedal and the "soft" pedal, which raises the dampers for only the keys that are pressed, making it possible for individual notes to be held as long as the pedal is pressed.

The piano has probably earned itself the reputation of being the most important instrument in musical history, mainly because of its enormous versatility. Virtually every significant composer has, at some time or other, written something especially for it, recognizing its enormous strength in both the concert hall and the relative intimacy of the drawing room or salon. It is also true that the best piano writers were, by necessity, fine pianists themselves, and wrote not only for their own performances but for their own virtuosity! Mozart provides the earliest evidence of this. As a child, he was known primarily for his extraordinary talents at the keyboard. He read difficult pieces at eight, improvised

69

Artur Rubinstein is considered to be one of the finest pianists of the twentieth century, and is famous for his interpretation of romantic works. He has played with almost every major orchestra throughout the world.

exquisitely, and generally performed so masterfully that when he played in Vienna at the age of six, his father, Leopold, wrote of his son: ". . . everyone says that his genius is incomprehensible."

At this early age, Mozart was beginning to create a collection of piano sonatas with violin accompaniment. But because of the young composer's remarkable ability to improvise, few of these were ever written down. At this time, too, he was composing his carefully-tailored sonatas solely for the piano—partly for self-performance and partly to earn a living. The piano, remember, was still new. It is not surprising, therefore, that of the more than forty concertos that Mozart wrote, twenty-three were for the keyboard. (Four early arrangements for piano and orchestra are now considered concertos, bringing the total to twenty-seven.) These, and the sonatas, form not only the two most important groups in the composer's prodigious output, but constitute his most original contributions to the evolution of music as well.

The Stein piano which Mozart liked had smaller hammers and lighter strings than you'd expect to find in a piano today. In his book on Mozart interpretations, Paul Badura-Skoda says the sound it probably made was "extraordinarily thin, translucent, sharply defined and silvery." Therefore, when we hear Mozart played today, we must listen through and beyond the full, rich, dark tones of the concert grand and try to recapture in our minds the world of sound which Mozart himself once knew as a world-famous concert pianist—at seven!

Like Mozart, Beethoven was considered one of the foremost virtuosos of his day. He is reputed to have performed everything he wrote except his fifth and last piano concerto, *Emperor*. The first performance of this work, on November 28, 1811, fell to a local pianist called Friedrich Schneider. At its important debut in Vienna (at a benefit concert for the Society of Noble Ladies of Charity), it was played by one of the composer's former students, Karl Czerny. Historians have since surmised that it was Beethoven's increasing deafness that deterred him from performing the work on both occasions, though it is a matter of record that he played the piano publicly long after these concerts. A London critic said in 1820 that, beginning in 1812 and extending to the end of his career, Beethoven's playing had become technically rough. His *Emperor Piano Concerto*, imperious, regal and grandiose—and certainly

71

one of his finest Romantic works—was beyond his talents.

Whereas Mozart and Beethoven enjoyed performing publicly, Frédéric Chopin (1810-1849) hated it. He claimed it made him both nervous and self-conscious, and he gave only thirty concerts in his entire career—although he was considered not only one of the finest pianists of his day but one of the greatest of all time.

The music Chopin wrote moved people to call him "the poet of the piano," and in his case it was a fitting label. He was a master of the short piano piece, the lyrical expression of romantic emotion, and was able to fuse melody, rhythm and harmony into the compass of an intense, mood-creating, evocative work. His name is forever associated with the salons of the French aristocracy during the era of Louis-Philippe, and his music captures everything that the refined sensibility of that gilded age connotes.

Chopin was particularly noted for his mazurkas, polonaises, nocturnes, preludes and etudes.

Mazurka: A country dance popular in Poland in the eighteenth and nineteenth centuries. It is moderately fast and usually in either 3/4 or 3/8 time, accented on the second or third beat. Chopin, the first composer to adapt the mazurka to concert music, went on to write more than fifty, all more or less following the style of the original dance.

Polonaise: The French word for "Polish." A stately court dance in 3/4 time, the polonaise originated in eastern Europe. Composers like Couperin and Telemann who wrote in the Rococo style used the polonaise as the basis for small orchestral suites. Bach also used it. But since those early days, the dance has taken on more elaborate rhythms, as is evident in Chopin's thirteen polonaises.

Nocturne: A slow, quiet and lyrical piece of music normally depicting night. The Irish composer-pianist John Field (1782-1837) wrote several pieces called nocturnes, and it is thought that Chopin borrowed the term from him. Other composers who used the title include Debussy and Fauré. Chopin wrote nine nocturnes for the piano.

Prelude: A name given to a composition which precedes a larger work. Preludes have been written to operas or to church services in the form of short organ works. Bach wrote forty-eight preludes to precede each of the forty-eight fugues in his keyboard collection, *The Well-Tempered Clavier.* Chopin, however, wrote twenty-four preludes as independent pieces, and Debussy, Scriabin and Shostakovich used the form too.

Etude: A piece of music written primarily to give finger exercise to a pianist. (Etude is a French word meaning "study.") Chopin wrote etudes which combine superb musical combination and opportunities for arduous practice. They are invariably included in the concert pianist's repertoire.

Audiences have been thrilled for almost a century and a half by the poetry of Chopin's music—the poignant harmonies, the plangent rhythms and the enduring melodies. Yet Chopin's fame in his day stemmed only from his private performances for select audiences, hence T.S. Eliot's lines:

Frédéric Chopin, the Poet of the Piano, disliked performing in public. He claimed it made him nervous and self-conscious. So, despite the fact that he was considered one of the finest concert pianist of his day, he gave only thirty concerts. As a composer, however, he was extraordinarily prolific.

> So intimate, this Chopin, that I think his soul
> Should be resurrected only among friends,
> Some two or three, who will not touch the bloom
> That is rubbed and questioned in the concert room.

Frédéric Chopin was Polish-born but French by adoption. Although he remained enamoured of his first love, the wealthy Delphine Potocka, and saw her frequently and in secret, he lived for ten years with a wealthy French noblewoman—a writer, Aurore Dudevant, who is credited with shaping the young composer's life.

Aurore, who was five years older than Chopin, wore trousers, smoked cigars incessantly, and to gain acceptance as an author, used a man's name—George Sand. She was a passionate and energetic woman, but after a year, the relationship mellowed to that of brother and sister. Then Chopin, who weighed a mere ninety-seven pounds, fell ill. The couple sought a warmer climate in Majorca, only to find themselves evicted from a hotel when it was thought Chopin had cholera. He and George took up residence in a disused monastery which, damp though it was, gave the composer an atmosphere

73

conducive to creativity. Indeed, he enjoyed there the most productive few months of his life. The later years were spent partly in Paris and partly on George Sand's property at Nohant. Having greatly influenced colleague Romanticists with daring harmonies in nearly 200 piano compositions, Chopin died at thirty-nine from tuberculosis.

Franz Liszt (1811-1886) was another eminent pianist-composer of his day. So far as his piano technique is concerned, there is evidence that he was even greater than Chopin. And while the modest Chopin preferred to perform privately, Liszt earned a reputation for his concert work. His audiences were always crowded with women; for them, the romantic character of the Hungarian composer had an irresistible attraction. Indeed, so great was Liszt's magnitude as a pianist, that a critic who was reporting on a concert he gave in 1824 said, "... the members of the orchestra were so enthralled by his playing that they forgot to pay attention to their own parts."

Franz Liszt earned a reputation for giving concerts that were invariably crowded with women enthralled by his romantic character and magnificent piano compositions. He was considered the finest pianist of his day.

After having toured Europe extensively as a boy, Liszt lost interest in performing, became lonely, and turned to religion for comfort. Despite a letter from his father which said, "You belong to Art and not to the Church," Liszt immersed himself in the Bible and other religious books and read them day and night until his health was affected. Later, though, when he was sixteen, the young composer discovered the truth of his father's words. He fell in love.

There appears to have been several lovers thereafter, one of whom was the young Countess Marie d'Agoult who, at twenty-two, left her husband and children and went home to Genoa with Liszt. The relationship lasted six years and left an important mark on the composer's life. Not only did the Countess bear him three children (their only daughter, Cosima, became Wagner's second wife), but through literary and artistic interests, helped him widen his general education. This, in turn, manifested itself in Liszt's art—especially when he returned to the concert platform.

Countess Marie d'Agoult became an author later, under the pseudonym of Daniel Stern. In her memoirs she wrote of her life with Liszt. "Strong affinities of race and temperament brought us together," she said, "but the extreme difference in our education and station in life necessarily raised innumerable difficulties between us, which finally made it impossible for us to live together."

Liszt wrote more than 1,300 compositions, most of them for the piano. He also made a valuable contribution to the development of music by using his powers as a superb orchestrator—a talent Chopin did not possess.

It was Liszt who introduced the symphonic poem or tone poem, as it is often called.

Symphonic poem: A large work for orchestra, invariably as long as a symphony but lacking the true symphonic form with movements. It is usually an interpretation of an extra-musical subject—a literary work, a painting, an historical event, even a geographic location. Liszt wrote a series of symphonic poems between 1850 and 1860. More popular examples of this musical unit are Sibelius' *Finlandia*, Smetana's *My Country*, Debussy's *La Mer*, Respighi's *Pines of Rome* and *Fountains of Rome*, Richard Strauss' *Don Juan* and Berlioz' *Symphony Fantastique*.

While Liszt, Chopin, Beethoven and Mozart emerge as, perhaps, the most illustrious, prolific and original writers for the piano, the instrument was used exceptionally well by Franz Schubert, not only in his vast collection of songs, of which only 634 have been preserved, but in his many piano sonatas. Concerto writers Schumann, Brahms and Rachmaninoff are also considered important composers for the piano.

Suggested Listening:

Suggesting specific pieces for listening from the vast collection of piano literature would be ludicrous, to say the least. It might, however, be useful to hear the contrasting uses composers, from Bach in the Baroque period and Schoenberg in the twentieth century, made of keyboard instruments. In passing, it might also be interesting and advantageous to note how many of the eminent composers used the sonata form, both in the concerto and the solo piano piece. Mozart's piano works, from childhood to maturity, for example, show a marked growth. Beethoven's five piano concertos show a similar development, the last two being distinctly darker and more heroic than the first three, which were more Classical and Mozart-influenced.

Opera

(8) *its origin, the rise of the virtuoso singers, formalized opera, Gluck's reform operas, Mozart and the move to freer form, Romantic opera, Wagner, Verdi, Puccini, Debussy, twentieth-century opera*

Many people dismiss opera on the basis that its stories are too far-fetched. But nothing could be more unfair. If we challenge credibility gaps, then we must dismiss half the world's finest literature. It is unlikely that an actual professor would have spent so much time inflicting elocution lessons on a hopeless flower girl as did Professor Higgins in George Bernard Shaw's *Pygmalion*, or that he would have involved himself in a class struggle in the entrance to a church. And in real life H.G. Wells' *Mr. Pyecroft* would never have been punished for his hypochondria by being made to spend his remaining years upside-down on the ceiling! Opera, then, must be accepted as a stylistic art and one which is traditionally performed at a theatrically high level of feasibility.

Obviously, people do not sing to each other in the course of their normal daily lives. But if we can accept characters breaking into song on trains and in elevators and court houses in musical comedies, why not in opera? After all, opera was the forerunner of musical comedy and has survived as an art combining two dramatic forces—the power of the visual and the power of music. Good opera uses these elements well, compensating for what may be, by today's reckoning, stories that are as implausible as they are silly.

Even the silliest stories, however, can have their human values, and Verdi's *Rigoletto* is a supreme example of this. The opera tells of a hunchback court jester, scorned for his appearance, who is the victim of a cruel trick whereby a wealthy Duke seduces his beautiful young daughter, Gilda. The same story, though in less theatrical terms, is not uncommon today. People the world over are often dismissed as vagrants and denied their human rights simply because they lack eloquence and cannot afford a collar and tie.

Puccini's *La Bohème* is another tragic opera, but more recent. Set at Christmas time, it finds a group of students unable to afford fuel for their attic fireplace, let alone a seasonal meal. Rodolfo, a poet, sacrifices his manuscript in the early stages of the opera to provide a little warmth. Later, he falls in love with the girl downstairs, against an emotional backcloth not unfamiliar to impoverished students today. This makes *La Bohème* particularly relevant to young people in the twentieth century, and one of the most frequently performed works in the operatic repertoire.

Opera is an Italian word meaning "work," but in English-speaking countries it has come to mean "musical work." Actually, an opera is simply a play set to music with all the ingredients thereof—acting, costumes, lighting, scenery, often ballet, and always musical accompaniment—except that the characters sing instead of speak. Whereas actors are given speeches to establish important moments in a play and singers in a musical comedy are given songs, singers in an opera are given arias. It is these arias that provide the climaxes in opera and give audiences some of the most lusty and haunting tunes ever written.

Although the birth-date of opera is considered to be 1600, when Jacopo Peri's *Euridice* was performed in Florence, combinations of dramatic action and music were being staged as early as the Middle Ages. These, and plays written during the early Renaissance, with a chanting or reciting chorus similar to the chorus in an

77

ancient Greek drama, are thought to be the forerunners of opera as we have come to know it today.

Early operas, like early music generally, were liturgical in character, and the instrumental accompaniment was simple in the extreme, often including only three or four flutes or pipes. But then, in line with religious beliefs, music was considered the entire servant of word. As time moved on, however, and as music evolved, orchestras became more important—and bigger. By the same token, increasing demands were made upon the skill and virtuosity of the players.

Similar demands were made on singers, and this manifested itself, in the very early stages of opera, in the birth of a vocal style called *coloratura* (colouring). This called for the singing of long passages on a single syllable with all kinds of trills and decorations. Coloratura passages were not usually written down by the composer, but improvised by the singer. As the art of singing developed, performers were eventually able to dictate to foremost opera composers like Monteverdi, Alessandro Scarlatti and Lully how they should write. Indeed, tyrant singers saw themselves at the centre of interest in opera, in place of the music, and it was not uncommon for a performer to refuse a role unless it displayed both the voice and the dramatic possibilities. One famous singer, Marchesi, even insisted, in his later years, upon making his entrance either high above the stage or on horseback!

During this eighteenth-century period of emphasis upon the performer, there emerged a type of opera consisting of separate songs in mixed musical form. The dialogue, which served to carry along the action, was sung in a terse, chanting style (called "recitative") and was usually accompanied by simple chords on the harpsichord *(recitativo secco)*. The more dramatic parts, however, were accompanied by the entire orchestra *(recitativo accompagnato)* and the moods of the characters were expressed in arias. Besides these solos, there were various forms of combined singing, from duets and quartets to larger ensemble scenes. The last scene of each act was invariably played on a large scale, visually and musically, and included the entire cast—principals and chorus. In all scenes, most attention was paid to the demands of musical form. Even when the situation required action and speed, the plot would be held up while the number was completed in its proper form. There were also fixed forms for orchestral passages.

One of the first operas to incorporate ballet was a tragedy, Alceste, by the French composer Lully. This engraving depicts the première performance at Versailles in 1674. True to the Baroque style, the stage was lit from above by thousands of candles.

A scene from the 1972 National Arts Centre's production of Mozart's Cosi fan tutte, with Allan Monk (Guglielmo), Patricia Wells (Fiordiligi), Rosalind Elias (Dorabella) and John Stewart (Ferrando). The conductor was Mario Bernardi.

Before the curtain rose, an overture was played, and in some of the French operas of this period ballet was included.

These early developments took place, for the most part, in Italy and France, where opera was not only supported by the courts of princes and nobles, but often written especially for festive occasions. The splendour of the staging and costumes played an important part, and gave the Baroque architects every opportunity to display their ingenuity.

The first public opera performed commercially opened in Venice in 1637 and was financed by wealthy families. Shortly afterwards, an Italian opera was staged in Paris. Vienna soon followed, and then England—first with Purcell, at the end of the seventeenth century and later with Handel. Handel was to become one of the most eminent masters of the early Italian style.

In the first half of the eighteenth century, two types of opera evolved. First, there was the serious, often tragic *opera seria* and second, the more popular, farce-like *opera buffa*. Beside the fun-provoking lightness and satire of *opera buffa*, the heavy *opera seria* appeared crude, artificial and unnatural. There was strong reaction against it, and in this Christoph Willibald von Gluck (1714-1787) was largely instrumental. He introduced his famous reform operas in which he aimed to abolish all that was unnatural, heavy and unnecessarily stilted and ornamental in Italian opera. First to disappear were the undramatic, repetitive arias and the unnecessary *coloratura*.

At first, Mozart followed Gluck's ideas in *opera seria*. His best known works, however, are a development of the *opera buffa* style plus strong influences of the light, operetta-like German style called *Singspiel*. Clearly, Mozart's aim was to make the music serve the poetry in the text rather than the other way round. He retained the idea of having opera consist of separate songs, but did not return to the stilted method of expression. As forcibly as Gluck, he demanded that the art should be natural. At the same time, he sought to avoid all that was stiff, dry and unconvincing in Gluck. With his far greater musical talent, he was able to achieve it—by joining Italian beauty of sound to Gluck's pathos, by developing the orchestra symphonically, by giving life to the old recitative, and by making the ensemble scene the crux of the opera and building up powerful symphonic finales. Indeed, Mozart created works so musically, psychologically and dramatically rich that they are unique in the history of opera.

French *opéra comique* developed from *opera buffa* and, like the *Singspiel*, contained spoken dialogue. This distinguished it sharply from grand opera, an extension of the *opera seria* style, which came into fashion during the Napoleonic Age, with Donizetti, Rossini, Spontini and Cherubini among its leading exponents. Beethoven's only opera, *Fidelio*, reveals the influence of French grand opera, but also looks forward to the next period, the Romantic era, initiated in Germany by Carl Maria von Weber.

Weber's operas bear all the characteristics of the Romantic period. He liked forest scenes and supernatural agencies and powers *(Der Freischuetz)*, enthusiasm for medieval chivalry *(Euryanthe)*, and mermaids and elves in an Oriental setting *(Oberon)*. His works still contained separate, individual forms and scenes, but they tended to overlap or even "slide" into each other more than did the scenes in earlier works. Furthermore, the part of the chorus was more natural and better motivated. Weber took German folk songs as models for his solos, and his orchestra painted the changing scenes and moods clearly and vitally with a refined use of instrumental colours.

Opera assumed the traits of Romanticism in other European countries in the works of such Nationalistic Romantics as the Czech Smetana and the Russians Glinka, Tchaikovsky and Mussorgsky.

One feature introduced by Gluck and Mozart, which later came into prominence in Romantic opera generally, was the new type of overture, of which the sonata form as developed by the Viennese Classical composers became the accepted framework. To an increasing extent, composers used tunes from the opera itself as themes, so that the overture developed into a symphonic poem, with the story of the opera as its programme.

In France, grand opera and *opéra comique* developed side by side. Grand opera, with the German-born Meyerbeer as its leading exponent, became an historical, scenic opera, in which effect was the main objective. *Opéra comique* gradually became more Romantic in character, under such composers as Boieldieu, Auber and Thomas. Gounod's *Faust* was essentially *opéra comique*. Its first form had spoken dialogue, but with the addition of important elements from grand opera. Bizet's *Carmen* broke almost completely with the sentimental Romantic *opéra comique*, and introduced an often extreme realism. Nevertheless, stylistically the work has more in common with *opéra comique* than with grand opera.

The history of opera in the second half of the nineteenth century is marked by two composers of genius—Wagner, a convinced revolutionary with his own ideas about the "art of the future," and the Italian Giuseppe Verdi (1813-1901), an evolutionist whose work was based on a more refined and intuitive feeling for the demands of dramatic music.

Romantic opera probably reached its culmination in the works of Wagner. He initiated musical dramas, for which he wrote his own librettos, and no one has since been able to imitate them. *Lohengrin*, his first, and *Parsifal*, his last, not only completely ignored the old number system, but violated it blatantly. These works are continuous in character—unifying music and drama as it had never been unified before.

Verdi, on the other hand, often returned to old methods. Hence there is invariably space after an aria, duet or ensemble scene for audience applause. He made other contributions to the advancement of opera though. His long musical life, from early works like *Rigoletto, Il Trovatore* and *La Traviata* to *Falstaff*, which he composed at eighty, was a steady and comprehensive development.

Verdi began in the traditional Italian *bel canto* style, and his great ability to create beautiful tunes was soon apparent. He possessed a rare gift for melody, and artistically he always tried to avoid what was conventional in the opera of his time. He was not interested in literary finesse, but nevertheless knew how to bring out the intense emotions and passionate feelings of human beings through his unfailing dramatic sense and his exceptional skill in musical characterization. As he developed, he became more particular in his use of effects. He then saw importance not in theatrical effects but in dramatic truth—and in humanity. This is clearly apparent in his operas composed in the 1850's—*Il Trovatore, Rigoletto* and *La Traviata*. In his later works he increased the compactness of the dramatic structure, and used the orchestra more symphonically. In time, he began to insist on better librettos.

After Verdi, there appeared in Italy a movement which demanded that life should be presented realistically on the operatic stage, instead of the heroic, exalted life portrayed by the libretti of the preceding operas.

82

One of grand opera's most stirring moments— the famous triumphal scene from Verdi's masterpiece, Aida, set in ancient Egypt. The photograph shows the Canadian Opera Company during a performance of the work in 1972, with Maria Pellegrini (Aida), Pedro Lavirgen (Radames), Don Garrard (Ramfis), Claude Corbeil (King), and Cornelis Opthof (Amonasro).

Coloratura arias were abandoned. Mascagni, Leoncavallo and Giordano belonged to this school of thought. Puccini was also a realist in some of his operas, but *La Bohème* and *Madame Butterfly* show more affinity with French lyrical opera, as represented by Massenet.

In the copious output of Richard Strauss there is to be found both a strong affinity with, and a strong reaction against, Wagner. *Salome* and *Elektra* are influenced by the large dimensions of Wagner's dramatic form, while *Der Rosenkavalier* harks back to the charm, clarity and grace of Rococo opera. In *Ariadne auf Naxos*, Strauss created a chamber opera which introduced a number of experimental features and showed his interest in the style of earlier ages.

In France, Debussy's *Pelléas et Mélisande* was of epoch-making importance. Here the dialogue was spoken rather than sung, but with a sense of intonation that made the work a unique document for the study of French speech. With its serenity, refinement and subtlety, and its Impressionistic method of expression, *Pelléas* represents a direct reaction against Wagner. There are no overwhelming masses of sound, shrieks of joy or despair. Debussy created intensity by suggestion, and replaced the massively passionate with delicate shades of emotion. Yet Debussy offered a solution to the problem

83

of opera that is almost identical with Wagner's. His songs are also "speaking songs"; his orchestra is symphonically constituted. *Pelléas et Mélisande* could hardly be said to have formed a school. But it influenced later composers; it helped to set them free from Wagner on the one hand, and Puccini on the other.

The twentieth century has been a period of conflict in opera—as in other musical forms. We have had Expressionism, Neo-objectivism and Neo-classicism, bitonality, polytonality and, at length, atonality. We have had operas with giant orchestras, and chamber works with orchestras of twelve or fifteen pieces.

Leading composers like Stravinsky, Hindemith, Honegger, Milhaud, Prokofiev, Shostakovitch and Schoenberg have all written works for the stage. Common to all of them is an attempt to move away from the broadly planned, symphonic drama and to approach a more theatrical opera. Among the most remarkable of the works of this age are Alban Berg's *Wozzeck*, an opera in which each scene is written in a strict musical form; Milhaud's grand operas, *Christophe Colombe* and *Bolivar;* Honegger's mystery play, *Joan of Arc at the Stake;* Gershwin's Negro opera, *Porgy and Bess;* Benjamin Britten's grand opera, *Peter Grimes,* and chamber opera, *The Rape of Lucretia;* and Gian-Carlo Menotti's chamber operas, *The Medium, The Telephone,* and *The Consul.*

A scene from the Canadian Opera Co.'s performance of Louis Riel, a new Canadian opera by Harry Somers, libretto by Mavor Moore and Jacques Languirand. One of the features of the opera was the use of film projected on hanging screens.

84

Jazz

(9)
its beginnings, work songs, spirituals, blues, ragtime, jazz centres: New Orleans, Chicago and New York, jazz styles

Although you may enjoy it and, to a certain extent "feel" it, you may never know the true depths and meanings of jazz unless you are black. Jazz began to be developed in the pits of poverty and misery in the United States towards the end of last century, although its precise place and date of origin has remained one of the biggest musical mysteries. It is thought, however, that it probably began in the music of African natives.

There is even some speculation about the exact meaning of the word "jazz." Some hold that it comes from a Creole word meaning "to speed up," and some say it is a derivative of the French *jaser* (to chatter). Another theory is that it is an abbreviation of "Jasbo," the first name of a Negro musician who pounded the bar pianos of the Deep South around 1900.

One thing more definite, however, is that the first cargo of slaves for the plantations of the United States crossed the Atlantic from Africa in 1620. Snatched from a society in which music played an important part both in religion and daily life, these slaves were soon singing in the cotton fields. Their music was characterized by the predominance of rhythm and by transitions from song to speech that were scarcely noticeable.

In the New World, music continued to form an essential part of Negro living. Eventually it spread from the plantations, and was adopted in all aspects of life, including the bars and the churches. Soon it became apparent that the Negro workers had taken the hymns of the white man and combined them with the music they had brought with them. The result was a repertoire of work songs, spirituals and blues that had, on one side, the indigenous characteristics of Africa, and on the other side, strong influences of the Wesleyan hymns of the Methodist revival.

Work songs: These were sung to lighten the gruelling manual work of the plantations. The Negroes sang as they worked, just as they had in Africa. Words and tunes were both improvised.

Spirituals: The Negroes sought consolation in Christianity, which promised them freedom from earthly misery. These genuinely religious Negro songs were closely related to African ritual, generally developing as a half-improvised exchange between a leader and a congregational chorus:
Leader: I got a robe.
        You got a robe.
Chorus: All God's chillun got a robe;
        When I get to Heab'n gonna put on my robe
        Gonna shout all over God's Heab'n.

Blues: The subjects of "blues" songs were drawn from both works songs and spirituals, and revealed in their musical forms the African's unfamiliarity with European harmony.

The "blues" are thought to have been the foundations of jazz as we know it today and although they have survived in their original form, they have led to other musical styles of which ragtime is one.

Based upon rhythm without any appreciable melody, ragtime originated in the attempts of Negro pianists in New Orleans to copy the brass band's trick of shifting the accent from the strong to the weak beat when playing march tunes. It was the ragtime tunes of the St. Louis composers Tom Turpin (*Harlem Rag*, 1895), Scott Joplin (*Maple Leaf Rag Time*, 1899) and others that made ragtime popular all over the United States in the 1890's. These composers found the inspiration for their tunes in the cakewalks of the Negroes, and the polkas, quadrilles, minuets and waltzes which were fashionable then in New Orleans, Memphis and St. Louis. They added typical Negroid rhythmic complications in conflict with the 2/2 or 4/4 time.

The peculiarities of ragtime are:

❖ lively, syncopated and incessant rhythm;
❖ exclusive connection with the piano.

It is also important to note that ragtime is characterized by the regularly-accented beat in the bass and extravagant syncopation in which lies the key to all Negro music—and thus to jazz. Pure ragtime for the piano continued to exist independently, while ragtime as a musical style became the dominant feature of the first jazz orchestras. (The jazz of this period is often referred to as ragtime; the word "jazz" was first used in Chicago about 1916.) Around 1910, however, attempts were being made to introduce simple melody—tunes taken from works songs, spirituals and, particularly, "blues." Hence, the old ragtime music became merely an accompaniment for a new composition in three layers:

❖ a fixed, almost march-like rhythm in the bass which tirelessly beat out the tempo;
❖ a lively and rhythmically-shifting syncopated accompaniment over the top of the bass;
❖ above these two a simple, singable melody.

One of the most important cities in the development of jazz was New Orleans. From the time of its foundation in 1718, New Orleans was a social checkerboard. Rich colonists hired impoverished slaves. God-fearing Catholics helped street-walkers and drunkards. Upright business men met adventurers and scoundrels from all parts of the world. The amusement centre was the district of Storyville which, until the end of last century, boasted more than two hundred dance halls and barrel houses, ranging from establishments which were luxuriously equipped to sinister dives. It was in this seedy, vicious atmosphere that jazz flourished and developed.

Because New Orleans had few racial prejudices it was not surprising that after the abolishment of slavery in 1865 thousands of Negroes went there to find work. Many became barbers, but others became musicians and acquired wind instruments discarded after the Civil War by the white military bandsmen. Since no one would teach them to play these instruments, the Negroes discovered a style of playing all their own.

In time, more and more Negroes found work as Storyville musicians playing in parade bands by day and in the halls by night. Buddy "Kid" Bolden was one of them. He was a cornettist, but he also had a dance band, Onward, which attracted enormous attention by performing not only normal dance tunes of the day— quadrilles, polkas and waltzes—but new ragtime numbers which were simultaneously and collectively improvised with some astonishing contrapuntal and polyrhythmic effects. Because a freely improvised style is the earmark of real jazz, Bolden's band has since been considered the very first jazz ensemble.

Apart from improvisation, the main characteristic of the New Orleans style of jazz was the combination of cornet, clarinet and trombone. Furthermore, Negro playing was always "vocal." Negroes called their instruments "voices" and tried to "sing" with them—just as they had once sung on the plantations. Intonation varied from a soft *glissando* to the so-called "dirty tone," a rough sound made by vibrating the tongue or soft palate. This type of improvised jazz was, thereafter, termed "hot" as opposed to "straight" jazz played from an arrangement written down beforehand.

Another important jazz pioneer in New Orleans was the trumpeter Manuel Perez who, according to some experts, initiated the new style even earlier than Bolden. These two men soon found themselves in competition with such ensembles as the Olympia Band and the Original Creole Orchestra—and eventually the white orchestras of the city which tried, more or less successfully, to imitate Negro jazz.

This saw the birth of Dixieland, a style generally used for jazz and played in quasi-New Orleans style by white musicians. It was begun by the ragtime band of Jack Laine, generally regarded as the father of white jazz music. The first white orchestra to venture outside Louisiana was Tom Brown and His Dusters, which played in Chicago in 1914. The following year saw the inception of the most famous white orchestra of all, the Original Dixieland Jazz Band, which performed at Schiller's Café in Chicago and later went to New York and Europe. By 1919, though, it was completely dominated by black musicians, and in 1925 it was dissolved.

Meanwhile, Chicago had witnessed a significant event in jazz history. When all the night spots of Storyville were closed down on November 12, 1917, by order of the United States' government, jazz was without a home. Some of the musicians stayed in New Orleans and others found work on the Mississippi excursion boats. Most, however, after playing funeral marches in the streets of Storyville, headed for Chicago, where jazz was to enjoy one of its more brilliant periods.

Among these musicians was "King" Oliver. When Oliver formed his own orchestra shortly after his arrival in Chicago in 1918, musicians from all over the United States flocked to hear him. He caused a sensation in 1922 when he took a young second cornettist called Louis Armstrong, then twenty-two, into his orchestra and gave him some solos to play. By 1923 Oliver and his Creole Jazz Band were making recordings which are regarded today as models for all jazz aspirants.

Other significant performers of the Chicago period of jazz, in which the saxophone displaced the trombone and the rhythm section was strengthened by the piano, were Benny Goodman and "Pee Wee" Russell, both clarinettists, and the drummer Gene Krupa. They advanced the cult, and introduced it to such cities as St. Louis, Kansas City and New York. New York eventually became the new jazz centre. Here, jazz aimed to satisfy the tastes of high society. Larger orchestras were developed to play fashionable tunes in well-written but facile orchestrations, a style initiated in about 1920 by Ted Lewis, Ben Pollack and Jean Goldkette. Later, however, it was developed more successfully by Paul Whiteman who originated the so-called "symphonic jazz." Whiteman's greatest success, though, came in 1924 when he commissioned and launched George Gershwin's *Rhapsody in Blue*.

The American composer George Gershwin began his career as a rehearsal pianist for a New York dance troupe. He later became one of the greatest composers who ever lived. His major success was Rhapsody in Blue, a work that might be classed as a jazz piano concerto.

George Gershwin (1898-1937): American. Born into a poor Jewish family in Brooklyn. Managed to take piano lessons in his teens. Later worked for a Tin Pan Alley music publisher to "taste" music. Eventually became a rehearsal pianist for a dancing troupe. First song composed, "Swannee," which sold a million copies. *Rhapsody in Blue*, a kind of jazz piano concerto, and *Porgy and Bess*, an opera, are clearly among his best works.

89

Some of the giants of jazz. Clockwise from top left: Dave Brubeck, Louis Armstrong, Duke Ellington, Benny Goodman.

Wrote many musical comedies producing fine songs. Awarded the Pulitzer Prize for "Of Thee I Sing." Died after an operation for brain tumour. The movie, *Rhapsody in Blue*, tells of the sad life of one of the finest composers who ever lived.

The Wall Street collapse of 1929 and the economic slump that followed left its mark on the entertainment business in New York, and many pure jazz musicians were forced to seek economic safety in the larger, commercial orchestras. There they played "sweet" jazz, which had a soothing effect on shattered nerves. Tommy and Jimmy Dorsey, the Teagarden brothers, Eddie Lang and others all joined Paul Whiteman's Orchestra, which was engulfed in a prevailing style of music rarely affording solos. At this time too, other large orchestras were being formed to play "sweet" jazz by such prominent exponents as Fletcher Henderson and Duke Ellington. Henderson was experimenting then with jazz for even larger orchestras but some of his early efforts sound so stiff that it is not surprising a musician like Louis Armstrong soon ceased to perform them. Other musicians, including Coleman Hawkins, continued to work with Henderson, however, and the new style grew.

In 1935, Benny Goodman announced his orchestra was playing "swing"—a style developed earlier by Fletcher Henderson, but one which Goodman exploited to the full.

"Swing": This form of music is intended to be dance music but is distinguished from "sweet" music by leaving room for improvisation, though generally speaking, collective improvisations are omitted.

One result of Goodman's work was that the co-operation between black and white mucisians not only became common, but produced some superb artistic results—even while harsh words were being thrown at swing orchestras in general for being "too commercial" and abandoning authentic jazz forms.

Unquestionably, jazz has made a solid contribution to the evolution of music, mainly through rhythmic developments, a freer conception of tonality, harmonic enrichment, and a greatly increased understanding of the possibilities of orchestral instruments. Moreover, for the first time in hundreds of years, jazz has caused polyphony to be understood and loved by a wide public.

91

Even more important, perhaps, is the fact that jazz has reawakened interest in free improvisation and thus revived the old conception of a performer as not only an instrumentalist who can play the notes in front of him but an all-round musician.

As early as 1908 Debussy made use of ragtime rhythms in his *Golliwog's Cake-Walk* and again two years later in *Minstrels*. But this was long before the new Negro music began to have any extensive effect in Europe. A ballet, *Parade (Rag-Time du paquebot)*, by Eric Satie appeared in 1917, and a year later, Stravinsky had some sheets of ragtime music sent to him and was enchanted. The result was *The Soldier's Story* and *Ragtime for Eleven Solo Instruments*, in which Stravinsky made copious use of jazz rhythms. His example was quickly followed by younger composers, particularly in France, where Milhaud experimented with jazz rhythms in such works as the ballet *Le Boeuf sur le Toit* (1920) and his Negro ballet, *La Création du Monde*. Direct jazz influence is seen in Honegger's *Concertino for piano and orchestra* (1925), and in 1927 Ravel published a sonata for violin and piano with a second movement entitled *Blues*. The first jazz opera, *Jonny Spielt Auf* (Jonny Strikes Up), was composed in 1927 by the Austrian-born Ernst Krenek, an ardent supporter of twelve-tone music.

Jazz has many other forms and styles worth looking at:

Piano jazz: Apart from ragtime piano music, which pursued its own course since the beginning of jazz, there is another special piano style, "boogie-woogie," which has remained almost unchanged since the days of its most famous pioneer, Jimmy Yancey. Another style, which has "Jelly Roll" Morton and James P. Johnson among its pioneers, developed into the dynamic piano playing of "Fats" Waller, and was further refined by Art Tatum, Errol Garner and Oscar Peterson.

Vocal jazz: The great blues singers developed a special Negro way of singing, in which the voice "slides around" the words. The style has retained its character through all the changing jazz fashions, and was exploited by such notable vocalists as Ella Fitzgerald, Ethel Waters, Billie Holiday and Sarah Vaughan.

Close harmony: Good jazz is also expressed in "close harmony" singing. Harmony singing was originally cultivated as a means of whiling away the time in the barber saloons of New Orleans, and was later developed by groups of white singers like the Boswell Sisters and the Andrews Sisters, and by coloured groups like the Mills Brothers, the Three Peppers, Slim and Slam, and the Five Spirits of Rhythm.

"Scat": There has also arisen among jazz musicians the characteristic vocal style known as "scat singing," in which noises take the place of words. This is said to have been started by Armstrong, and was taken up by the "Hi-de-ho" King, Cab Calloway. It was also cultivated by Dizzy Gillespie and others in bizarre "be-bop" noises.

"Bop": Be-bop, re-bop, or plain bop was initiated during and just after the Second World War by pioneers of the older jazz generation, particularly Roy Eldridge, Charlie Christian, the saxophonist Les Young, and the drummer Kenny Clarke. Their first experiments took place at those chance meetings of musicians in restaurants, the so-called "jam sessions" which have long been a feature of jazz. Here arose a style with greater freedom for soloists, bolder and more imaginative harmonies and complicated rhythms, with the ground rhythm on the bass and constantly varying rhythmical figures on the cymbals, tenor drum and bass drum. Occasional passages in a more refined style are abruptly interrupted by violent quick passages with unmotivated and surprising accentuations.

"Cool": As a reaction against the turbulent bop style, some players turned to a more "cool" method of play-ing. Even in bop there was a tendency for the phrases of the melody to "hang behind" the beats of the ground rhythm. This tendency was carried further, and at the same time a change was made to a thinner tone, almost free from vibrato. The pianist George Shearing and his small chamber orchestra developed this slender and sober form. In the more poised and polished manner of playing thus inaugurated, the harmonies are spread as widely as possible in the "cool" style; every possibility of expanding the basic chord is exploited; the rhythm is built around the bass (in its lowest register) with a faint sliding accompaniment from brushes on the tenor drum. Stan Getz is a front-rank exponent of this style.

Progressive: In this extension of the bop music of the

larger orchestras, Latin-American influence is traceable, and sound effects are developed to the extreme. A prominent figure was the arranger Stan Kenton. Many connoisseurs insist that "progressive" is only a sideline, and that the true line of development runs through the "cool" style.

Many night clubs have small, informal jazz bands like this group in the Junkaroo Night Club, Nassau.

Suggested Listening:

Gershwin:	*Rhapsody in Blue, An American in Paris, Fascinating Rhythm.* Songs: "Lady Be Good," "Strike Up the Band," "Embraceable You," "Bess, You is My Woman Now" *(Porgy and Bess)*, "The Man I Love"
Duke Ellington:	"Solitude (1933), "Sophisticated Lady" (1933), "Satin Doll," "Caravan," "Mood Indigo"
W.C. Hardy:	"St. Louis Blues" (1914)
Hoagy Carmichael:	"Rockin' Chair" (1930), "Stardust" (1929)
Edward (Kid) Ory:	"Muskrat Ramble" (1925)
Dave Brubeck:	"Take Five,' "Pick Up Sticks," "Blue Rondo à la Turk"
Coleman Hawkins:	"Boff Boff"
Debussy:	*Golliwog's Cake-walk*

Musical Vienna

(10) Haydn, Mozart, Beethoven, Schubert, Brahms vs. Bruckner, the Strauss family, the operetta

Vienna's musical heritage dates back to the Middle Ages. In those days, the Augustinian canons and sects of monks like the Benedictines and the Cistercians sang Gregorian chants and learned musical theory in their schools, and Austrians generally always had an open door for the wandering, singing minstrel. But a time of even greater musical glory was to come. Within a forty-seven-year period (between 1781 and 1828) Vienna became firmly established not only as a musical drop-in centre but as a city which fostered the Classicists at their most prolific. Virtually the entire corpus of Classical music was written in or around the rooming houses and beer gardens of Vienna from the time Mozart took up permanent residence there on March 16, 1781, until the untimely death of Schubert on November 19, 1828.

Music in the classical vein, of course, was being composed earlier, but relatively half-heartedly and without the style of that which came later. The German opera reformer, Gluck, also a forerunner of the Classical period, went to Vienna in about 1736. But the task of shaping the style and determining the form of the new age was left to Joseph Haydn, who was allotted both a long life and a good sense of order and application with which to accomplish all he set out to do.

Haydn went to Vienna at the age of eight to sing in the choir of St. Stephen's Cathedral. When his voice broke, however, he was cast off and spent some years in a humble attic at 1220 Michaelerplatz, trying to make ends meet by offering, with his friends, impromptu, open-air concerts, which were then very much in vogue in upper middle-class and aristocratic circles. Haydn's first compositions were probably performed for such occasions. Later, he was commissioned by a comedian, Kurz-Bernadon, to write an opera, *Der krumme Teufel*, but this has not come down to posterity. In 1759, however, he obtained his first post in the service of the nobility, with Count Graz Morzin, and in 1761 he was engaged by Prince Esterházy as director of his private orchestra.

Nowadays, when social conditions are so different, there may be an inclination to regard Haydn's position in the Esterházy service as degrading—as an insult to an artist, especially since the announcement of his appointment stipulated he was to be "regarded and treated as one of the domestic staff." But, in fact, there was nothing at all degrading about either his position or the obligation to compose as occasion demanded. The prince respected Haydn, and in return, the composer was more than content, as is abundantly clear from his extraordinary output while he was there. As Haydn himself put it, "My employer was very satisfied with my work; I was commended, and with an orchestra at my disposal I could make experiments and observe which of them represented improvements and which not. I could make corrections and additions, cuts and innovations. I was cut off from the outside world, and there was no one to put me off or irritate me. I was forced to be original."

Prince Nicholaus Esterházy was himself an accomplished musician, and Haydn composed for him no fewer than 160 pieces for the baryton, one of the prince's favourite instruments. It was not until after the prince's death, in 1790, that Haydn became a free-lance composer. Two triumphal visits to England made him world-famous, and he was also treated as a celebrity in

Vienna—notably at the ceremonial performance of his fine oratorio *The Creation* before an audience comprising all the social and intellectual élite of Vienna. As he was escorted to his seat he was greeted by a fanfare of drums and trumpets, and at the wonderful passage "Let there be light," the whole audience applauded. Haydn, however, merely pointed heavenwards and said, "That is where my inspiration comes from."

Mozart chose a different road. In music he was a revolutionary, refused to submit to aristocratic patronage and cut himself off from the Salzburg Court where he earned his daily bread. In *The Marriage of Figaro* the embers of the French Revolution are clearly discernible as the servant succeeds in outwitting his lord and master. But the day when a composer could stand on his own feet had not yet dawned, and Mozart came to a lonely end, borne to a common grave in St. Mark's Cemetery in Vienna without a soul to accompany him. Of Haydn's funeral, on the other hand, his biographer Griesinger wrote: "Had it not been that the death of the great man occurred at a time when Vienna was too deafened by the tumult of war to have ears for anything else, the great concourse of his admirers would have arranged a magnificent funeral. As it was, the French authorities (Napoleon having occupied Vienna in this year of Haydn's death, 1809) announced his decease in the daily papers in a most honourable manner."

After the deaths of Mozart and Haydn, who lived as differently as their genius was akin, the main role in music in Vienna devolved upon Beethoven. He continued the development by making it subservient to his heroic will and his ethical aspirations. The personality great enough to apply himself to such a task obviously needed to be rooted in soil tougher than Vienna—or even Austria—had to offer. Yet, for the gradual blossoming and final blooming of such a personality, the musical atmosphere of the Imperial City was once again to prove indispensable.

The young Beethoven had already left his native Bonn before Mozart's death, seeing then—at only sixteen—outstanding differences between Vienna and other major European cities. Vienna was a centre of European culture in general—and music in particular. Moreover, it was girdled by graceful and inspiring hills—hills that had a special appeal to musicians, especially in the dawn of Romanticism, when a renewed interest in the natural beauties of nature was fashionable. The Viennese landscape, then, was one of the prime considerations that induced Beethoven, in whose personality a love of nature was paramount, to stay to compose virtually all his important works.

Picturesque Vienna also inspired the blazing genius of Schubert. By setting to music fine lyrical poems by such writers as Heine and Goethe, he created what we now consider the heart and soul of the entire output of *lieder*. True, he produced symphonies, masses, and piano and chamber music, but there is little doubt that his *lieder* are his finest contribution to music, representing the culmination of the *lieder* as a genre.

Franz Schubert, like Beethoven, was inspired by the atmosphere of Vienna. He set many fine poems to music, and left us a rich heritage of lieder.

There was something elemental about Schubert's emergence in Vienna as a *lieder* composer—something so unparalleled that we tend to overlook all that had gone before, and begin the history of the *lied* with him. But there were *lieder* in plenty long before Schubert's day, even as far back as the Baroque era in Vienna and, afterwards, in the days of Gluck. However, Schubert's songs have more dimension. Their essential features are their romantic feeling for nature and their wealth of emotion, as witnessed in the song cycles *Winterreise* and *Die schoene Muellerin*, in which an idyllic opening is gradually clouded by bitterness and resignation.

Schubert wrote *lieder* of an almost infinite variety, from the most elementary strophic song to complete settings, from recitative to ingenious variations of the melodic line, abounding in subtleties of all kinds. But it is, perhaps, the harmonies that constitute the final and most perfect means of expression, with the piano accompaniment asserting itself as an equal partner to the singer.

Hugo Wolf's brilliant lieder gave Austrian music a new life in the second half of the nineteenth century. Yet he did not compose anything important till he was nearly thirty.

The mission and vital impulse of Austrian music was by no means exhausted by Haydn, Mozart, Beethoven and Schubert. On the contrary, in the second half of the nineteenth century it was given new and different life by the symphonies of Johannes Brahms and Anton Bruckner (1824-1896) and the *lieder* of Hugo Wolf (1860-1903). But by then Austria could no longer claim absolute hegemony of the world of music. Richard Wagner had appeared in Germany and Giuseppe Verdi was busy in Italy. With their theatrics, these two were attracting world interest to their music-dramas and operas.

Meanwhile back in Austria, there was raging a musical drama fraught with the tension never before known in the development of an art. Brahms and Bruckner faced each other bitterly. Their colleagues and their enemies looked on. "If this nightmare caterwauling is the music of the future, which is impossible, then we do not envy the future," said the notoriously mordant critic Eduard Hanslick about Bruckner's *Eighth Symphony*. Hugo Wolf, a great champion of Wagner and Bruckner, expressed himself almost equally strongly. He called the critic Max Kalbeck, who was also in favour of Brahms and against Bruckner, a "journalistic guttersnipe," and opined that even one of Bruckner's minor works was "a Chimborazo compared to Brahms' symphonic mole-hills." The feud between the Wagnerites and the Conservatives, who had chosen Brahms as their champion, raged with an animosity that was at times distinctly unedifying. Today there are other problems over which to take sides, and the music of both Brahms and Bruckner is cherished.

Brahms' music—culminating in four symphonies, a requiem and a vast amount of chamber music, *lieder* and piano music—is the product of Romantic ideas tempered by respect for form and for the Classical tradition. It achieved recognition infinitely more readily than Bruckner's. But Bruckner's nine symphonies, three big masses and string quintet are steadily gaining respect and popularity the world over.

After the great symphonic composers came the Strausses, the most Viennese of all. They elevated light music, polkas, gallops and the fascinating airs of operetta to the realm of the sublime. So, too, did they influence the waltz, that swirling embodiment of vivacious merriment, once considered a highly questionable if not downright immoral activity. The waltz, after all, was the first dance where the partners embraced, and moralists railed against the abomination of "a lady permitting a man to encircle her with his arms and press the contour of her waist." Reformed dancing masters wrote graphic exposés, forthrightly revealing the ballroom for what it was—"A hotbed of vice within whose treacherous embrace so many sweet young souls have been whirled to perdition."

With recommendations like that, it was only a matter of time before the waltz became the rage of Europe . . . and nowhere did it catch on better than in glittering Vienna where Johann Strauss the Elder (1804-1849) was crowned the first Waltz King. As was properly befitting, the title was passed down from father to son—but not, it must be said, without a terrible battle on the part of the father. Johann the Elder had three sons: Johann Junior (1825-1899), Josef (1827-1870) and Eduard (1835-1916). The oldest boy started composing little waltzes when he was six and Johann the Elder became nervous. When his son began taking violin lessons he proceeded to more direct action. He told young Johann all manner of nasty stories about how a musician's life could be a struggling one, and when that failed he took away the boy's violin and locked it in a cupboard. He also forbade him to take lessons, and just to make sure that he didn't, packed him off to be a bank clerk.

The results were predictable. The more obstacles he found in his way, the more Johann Junior was determined to overcome them. He continued to take lessons (from his father's concert master, no less), and finally, in October 1844, when he was only nineteen, hired an orchestra and let all of Vienna know that he, too, was going into the music business.

Strauss the Elder was angry. First he tried to stop the concert, and when he found that he could not, he sent along a group of friends to hiss and boo and turn the debut into an embarrassing fiasco. But even that failed. The men starting making their rude noises on schedule, but the audience, captivated by the handsome Strauss Junior as he conducted with his violin bow, shushed them down. The crowd listened, applauded, and went on to greet the boy's musical magic with cheers and tears of joy. Just when it seemed that the fever of excitement could rise no further, Johann waved his arms for silence, turned to his orchestra, and then began conducting his father's most famous waltz—"Lorelei Rheine Echoes." That did it; the hall went wild, and the sentimental Viennese, even those who had originally come to ruin the performance, rushed forward, swept Johann up onto their shoulders, and carried him off in triumph.

From the moment of that glorious debut, Strauss' fame grew steadily. In all, he wrote about five hundred pieces, including such memorable works as "The Blue Danube," "Tales from the Vienna Woods," "Voices of Spring," "Artist's Life" and "Wine, Women and Song." When his father died from scarlet fever, there was no

Johann Strauss Senior was the first King of the Viennese Waltz. The new dance was the rage of Europe, and as its chief exponent he was much sought after.

longer any doubt who wore the Waltz King's crown. Johann immediately merged his own orchestra with his father's, and built up an organization numbering about two hundred people—copyists, musicians, singers, arrangers, assistant conductors and even press agents. At one point, Strauss had three different orchestras playing simultaneously at different Viennese ballrooms, with the maestro himself merely stopping in to make a brief appearance at each, and perhaps to conduct a waltz or two personally.

Strauss exalted the waltz, derived from the *laendler* (a country dance and ribald song popular in the Austrian and Bavarian Alps) into a real work of art. He brought to it bold harmonies, an artistic gusto, and an almost symphonic stature. The hallmarks of his compositions were the extra polish of their melodies, and the extraordinary richness of their content. It was Strauss, too, who suffused the waltz with that spirit of gay abandon, of longing and delight, which it has come to symbolize.

Even a composer like Wagner appreciated the waltz as an art form. "In charm, delicacy, and real musical content," he said, "one single waltz of Strauss towers above most of the mass-produced foreign stuff which we are at such pains to import." And another famous composer had something to add to the opening bars of a Strauss waltz inscribed on a woman's fan: "Unfortunately not written by me: Johannes Brahms."

Johann Strauss Junior displaced his father as Waltz King despite the latter's determined efforts to prevent it.

Although the Congress of Vienna made a notable contribution to the popularity of the Viennese waltz, the really decisive factors in its development were the works of Schubert and Weber. Schubert, with his German dances, *laendler* and waltzes, elevated the composition of waltzes onto a higher plane than ever before, while Weber, with his *Invitation to the Dance* (1819), laid down the standard form of the modern waltz.

The waltz was also a characteristic of Viennese operetta which, being the typical expression of middle-class culture in the days of Franz Joseph I, is a product of the second half of the nineteenth century. But operetta goes back to the *Singspiel*, more than a hundred years ago, and since Haydn and Mozart both influenced the development of *Singspiel*, it must be recognized that they are partially responsible for operetta. So, too, is the Frenchman Jacques Offenbach who wrote a series of *musiquettes*. The first performance of one of these Offenbach musiquettes, *Le Mariage aux Lanternes*, took

101

place on October 18, 1858. Another, *Orphée aux Enfers*, was produced in the same Carl Theatre in 1860.

But the first work to display all the typical characteristics of Viennese operetta (plenty of waltzes and a libretto adding extra polish to the topical satire of Offenbach's works) was *Das Pensionat* by Franz von Suppé. This had its world *première* at the Theatre an der Wien on November 24, 1860. It was followed by a string of operettas which made Suppé internationally known. These included *Flotte Bursche* (1863), *Die schoene Galathee* (1865), *Fatinitza* (1876) and *Boccaccio* (1879).

"You ought to write operettas, you've got all the qualifications," Offenbach once said to Johann Strauss. So Strauss duly replied. His first attempt, *Die lustigen Weiber von Wien*, was filed away and never heard again, but the first performance of *Indigo* in 1871 caused a furore. One of Vienna's leading critics in those days, Ludwig Speidel, wrote: "How charmingly coquettish the polkas and quadrilles are, how easy-going and convivial, how pointed and piquant! And in case the audience doesn't succumb to these spells, the wizard has another trick up his sleeve which never fails to come off—the waltz!" Another eyewitness gives an enthusiastic description of how one of the waltz-songs in *Indigo* brought down the house.

Ever since Johann Strauss' days, the waltz-song has been an integral feature of Viennese operetta. As Erich Schenk rightly emphasizes in his *Kleine Wiener Musikgeschichte*, "It was by instinctively giving pride of place to his waltz-songs, for which he had a gift all his own, that Johann Strauss asserted himself as a composer for the theatre too."

Indigo, now known as *The Thousand and One Nights*, was by no means Strauss' only successful operetta. Wagner once said of him: "He has more music in his head than anyone else in this century." *Die Fledermaus*, first performed on Easter Sunday 1874, was another spectacular success. In fact, of the eighty-eight operetta performances at the Theater an der Wien that year, fifty-eight were of *Die Fledermaus*. Even more prodigious, though, was the achievement of *Der Zigeunerbaron* (1885), which, during the winter, ran for eighty-five consecutive performances. The way Strauss set about composing *Zigeunerbaron* was characteristic: he wrote the music from the scenario and the actual text later.

Franz von Suppé had a long career as both composer and conductor. Today he is remembered chiefly for the overtures to Light Cavalry and Poet and Peasant.

The scenes on the opposite page are from D'Oyly Carte Company productions: at top—Act I of Ruddigore; at bottom— Act I of HMS Pinafore. Both operettas are by Gilbert and Sullivan.

If Johann Strauss can be said to have created the golden age of operetta, the fruitful years on either side of the turn of the present century merit at least the honorary title of silver age. The lilting 3/4 rhythm which was still the main ingredient of dance music had indeed slightly changed its measure and its proportions, and the instrumental waltzes of the Strauss era, which were written to be danced to, gave way to the waltz-songs of Franz Lehár, Oscar Straus, Leo Fall and Emmerich Kálmán. All these artists worked in Vienna, and it was from Vienna that *The Merry Widow*, the *Chocolate Soldier*, *The Girl in the Train* and the *Csárdásfuerstin*, with their haunting, sentimental tunes, started out on their journey round the world.

Other leading operetta composers of this period were Oscar Straus (*A Waltz Dream*, 1907); Leo Fall (*The Dollar Princess*, 1907, and *Madame Pompadour*, 1923); and Edmund Eysler (*Bruder Straubinger*, 1903, and *Die goldene Meisterin*, 1927). But the most successful of all the composers of the silver age of operetta was Franz

The famous writer of operettas, Franz Lehár, is shown here with the tenor Richard Tauber and the soprano Kathe Dorsch. Tauber, an Austrian, performed all of Lehár's leading tenor roles. Lehár, in turn, honoured Tauber by composing for him The Land of Smiles, one of his most popular works.

Lehár, some of whose operettas closely resemble the old *Singspiel* and *opéra comique*. Among his operettas that have established themselves in almost every country are *The Merry Widow* (1905), *The Count of Luxemburg* (1909), *The Czarevitch* (1928), and *Land of Smiles* (1930)—which he wrote especially for the tenor Richard Tauber. The chief reasons behind Lehár's success were his fund of melody, lilting rhythms, and effervescent vitality. The man who began as a bandmaster in the Hungarian army has gone down in history as one of the greatest masters of Viennese operetta.

Operetta continued to delight audiences—especially through such renowned and busy composers as the Austrian Robert Stolz, the Czechoslovakian Rudolf Friml and the Hungarian Sigmund Romberg. Stolz wrote the famous *The Whitehorse Inn*. Friml enjoyed success with *The Firefly*, *You're in Love* and the Canadian Rockies-inspired *Rose Marie*. Romberg won even greater acclaim with *The Desert Song*, *The New Moon* and *The Student Prince*. But it is more significant to note that all these works, even *The Student Prince* (1924), set against the academic backcloth of old Heidelberg, were written in adopted countries. Stolz moved to the United States in 1901, Friml in 1906 and Romberg in 1909. In so doing, these composers not only brought Viennese ways to North America, but introduced to Americans the possibility of creating musical theatre of their very own.

The response was eager. The Irish-born Victor Herbert, once a cellist at the Metropolitan Opera and married to a German singer in the same company, was also inspired to write pseudo-Viennese operetta. By the time of his death in 1924, he had written thirty-five, including *Babes in Toyland*, *The Red Mill*, and his most popular, *Naughty Marietta*, recently given a New York revival. Soon Americans were producing musical shows we now call musical comedies—light shows with spoken dialogues as well as solo songs, duets, trios, quartets and choruses, and, like operetta, usually incorporating dancing.

The main difference between musical comedy and operetta is simply one of musical trend. Whereas operetta was influenced by more "serious" Viennese music, musical comedy tends to be related more to jazz or popular music.

Irving Berlin, a successful musical comedy writer, started his career in 1911 at twenty-three, by having his song "Alexander's Ragtime Band" published. He then went on to compose both music and lyrics for a steady stream of musical comedies, including *Annie Get Your Gun, Call Me Madam* and *As Thousands Cheer.* Among his songs are: "Always," "Remember," "Easter Parade," "I'm Dreaming of a White Christmas" and "God Bless America."

Other well-known musical comedy writers are: Jerome Kern (*Show Boat, Sally, Sunny, Music in the Air* and *Very Warm for May*); Cole Porter (*Kiss Me Kate, Something for the Boys* and *Silk Stockings*); Richard Rogers (*Oklahoma, Carousel, South Pacific, The King and I, The Sound of Music* and *Flower Drum Song*); George Gershwin (*Lady Be Good, Strike Up the Band, Show Girl* and *Of Thee I Sing*); and, more recently, Leonard Bernstein (*Candide* and *West Side Story*).

Religious music

The most sublime expressions of artistic impulse have been associated with religion ever since the beginning of the human race. The colossal Pyramids and temples of ancient Egypt, on the one hand, and the towering Gothic cathedrals of the Middle Ages, on the other, document more than anything man's inherent desire to lavish his art freely upon a belief in a god. But these expressions have not merely been confined to architecture. Sculpture, with its statues and effigies, has been an assiduous handmaiden of religion. During the Middle Ages, especially, man spoke of God through paintings and the work of the silversmith, glassblower and weaver.

Musicians have served religion, too, with an eloquent devotion often unparalleled. As the Church has grown, so has its music. Again, the joy must be in the listening. The best and obvious way to recognize the musical characteristics of various faiths is by either attending services or listening to them whenever possible on the radio. There are fascinating discoveries to be made. You do not have to be religious to note the important personalities, developments and styles of Church music from the very earliest times.

Without question, the richest contribution to liturgical music has been made by the Roman Catholic Church, with its impressive architectural resources and rituals, and its lavish use of virtually every form of art and craftsmanship. Indeed, from its very birth, the Roman Catholic Church has sought to make its forms and symbols both beautiful and appealing. More recently, perhaps, its musicians have been accused of garish vulgarity. But they have, nonetheless, succeeded in clothing their doctrine in the fairest guise to make worship an aesthetic delight.

The most solemn rite among the various functions of the Catholic Church is the Mass, an elaborate development of the Last Supper, which dramatizes the fundamental doctrine of Christ's sacrifice for the remission of sins. Several kinds of Mass are used, differing in detail according to the functions they serve. There is the High Mass, Solemn High Mass, Low Mass, Requiem Mass, Votive Mass and others. The Requiem Mass represents the widest departure from the usual Mass form. In this we find the medieval judgement hymn *Dies Irae*, as well as certain prayers for the dead.

The Mass is fundamentally a musical service wherein words and music are inseparable. The musical service of the Catholic Church, though, has passed in general through the same stages as the entire development of musical art:

❖ unison chant
❖ unaccompanied choruses
❖ instrumental accompaniment

The unison chant constituted the only form of Church music from the beginnings of the Church in Rome to about A.D. 1100. It drew its sources from the ancient Greeks, Romans and Hebrews, and was developed to considerable maturity in the early monasteries of Syria, Chaldea and Egypt.

The biblical chants supplied the first texts, which came to be treated as:

❖ the psalmodic solo
❖ the responsive chant (solo and chorus)
❖ the antiphonal chant (two alternating choruses)

Then came those wordless, ecstatic jubilations known as alleluias, and finally, from these and the biblical chants, sprang up what was virtually a Christian folk song. From that day to this, the Christian folk song has never waned.

The Greek Church played an important part in the transmission of some of the major elements to the music of the Western Church. From the enormous mass of hymns poured forth by the early Greek hymn writers, many (such as the two Glorias, the "Gloria Patri" and the "Gloria in Excelsis," the "Ter Sanctus," or cherubic hymn heard by Isaiah in a vision, the "Te Deum," the "Magnificat," the "Benedictus" and the "Kyrie Eleison") were adopted by the Western Church and form the backbone of the whole ritualistic structure.

The Edict of Toleration by Constantine in 312, by which Christianity became the predominant religion of the Roman Empire, resulted in the rapid evolution and consolidation of the Church organization, and marked the final crystallization of the ritual and the complete assumption by the clergy of the musical worship. The ritual became priestly and liturgical. The laity ceased to participate in the musical office, and finally the whole responsibility devolved upon the carefully trained choristers drawn from the minor clergy. A highly organized body of chants came to constitute the substance of the musical service for a thousand years.

Pope Gregory the Great (590-604) has been credited with determining the liturgical chant. This included freeing the Church song of the fetters of Greek prosody, collecting the existing chants, adding others, providing them with a system of notation, and setting them down in the Antiphonary of St. Gregory. He also established a singing school, and added four new scales or modes to the four already recognized. It is thought that this work was undertaken by a large number of people, though nothing in Pope Gregory's voluminous correspondence bears this out.

The body of chants which has been handed down is enormous, comprising thousands of fine melodies. During the Church's evangelical periods, spanning the first eleven centuries of the Christian era, the plainsong was the chief crusading weapon. It served the same function as Luther's hymns in gaining recruits for the Reformed Church, or the patriotic songs of a nation girding its strength for war. The chant has always maintained an important place in the Catholic ritual despite its many upheavals and alterations.

The symbols of notation used during the period of the unison chant were called the "neumes," and numbered about thirty. This intricate system, intended mainly as a reminder for the experienced singer, indicated the proper rhythm, variations of tempo, embellishments, and style of delivery. Not until Guido of Arezzo (born in 995) discovered stave notations, could the art of composition be said to have really begun. Guido is also said to have invented the Ut-Re-Mi-Fa-So system (later developed into Do-Re-Mi-Fa-So-La-Ti-Do) to lighten the burden of young choir boys when they learned their chants.

Medieval music was unmeasured, lacked definite rhythmic pattern and tended to be made to fit the words. The next important step in the evolution of Church music was the invention, in France, of the discant (or descant), and the introduction of embellishments called "fleurettes." At first a discant contained only two parts—the lower sung by the tenor and the upper sung by the boy soprano. Later, other voices were added—the alto and the bass.

When three or four expert discanters sang together, inventing their own parts, mixing folk songs with chants, and singing in three or four different languages, the results may have been satisfactory. But when a whole chorus of unseasoned singers started discanting, the result was a veritable pandemonium. In the desperation of self-defence, musicians sought some medium of relief from this auditory torture, and finally managed to perfect a system of notation which would indicate the relative duration of notes. Thus arose *musica mensurata* (measured music), as opposed to *musica plana* (plain music).

Discant became the rage in France during the thirteenth century. Special schools were founded and choirs were formed to out-sing each other with a variety of complex effects. But by the end of the fourteenth century the monkish theories of musical puzzles, harmonic and rhythmic stiffness, and blind, lifeless formalism disappeared. These ruptures and innovations were auspicious heraldings of the advent of another age in Church music—the golden age, not to be confused with the golden age of opera, which occurred around the turn of the twentieth century.

The golden age of Church music, during the first part of the fifteenth century, brought radical inventions.

Counterpoint was being developed both in England and throughout Northern Europe. The result was the unaccompanied Mass and a deluge of hymns and magnificats, all seeking sweetness of expression. The period was called the golden age because it marked the climax of centuries of musical effort, and culminated in the development—chiefly through Orlando di Lasso, Palestrina and Giovanni Gabrieli—of the madrigal.

The Flemish maestro Lasso was undoubtedly the most prolific composer who ever lived. His output numbered 2,337 works! He wrote fifty-one masses, 516 motets, 180 magnificats, 429 sacred songs, and a mountain of ecclesiastical compositions: vespers, litanies, hymns, psalms, Passions and Stabat Maters. His secular compositions were also numerous, and included fifty-nine canzonettas, 371 French chansons and 233 madrigals! Lasso broke away from some of the more rigid rules of counterpoint, and wrote with greater fluency than most of his predecessors. His handling of modes was more flexible, and his voice parts were more florid and more directly expressive of human passions and feelings.

The practice of Lasso's noble patron was typical of a custom that grew up during this period. The more powerful sovereigns as well as the lesser rulers and great nobles established the *scholae palatinae*, imperial singing schools and choirs, which reached a high degree of artistic skill. The Chapel Royal of England was maintained by the royal house. The King of France, the Sforzas at Mantua, the Medici at Florence, the Estes at Milan, and numerous other great houses maintained elaborate choruses and schools, nearly all directed by Flemish maestros who were deemed the last word in musical competency at this period.

The Venetian master, Gabrieli, was the centre of a flourishing school in Venice. In Spain, T.L. de Vittoria (1540?-1613) vied with Lasso in his superb musicianship and indefatigable organizing skill, and is sometimes even ranked with Palestrina. France, too, had caught the spirit of the Flemish, and nourished a vigorous school of composers. Among them was Claude Guodimel, who taught Palestrina counterpoint.

Music of the Lutheran Church

Music of the Lutheran Church represents the individualistic spirit that fomented the schism and animated the organization of the Reformed Church. Whereas the

Catholic Church reduced the musical participation of the congregation to the minimum, and for centuries based its whole musical fabric upon the priestly Gregorian chant, the music of the Reformed Church was founded on the congregational hymn.

In the Catholic Church the clergy were the mediators between its adherents and God. In the Lutheran Church the congregation itself constituted a universal priesthood, with direct access to the seat of mercy. In the Lutheran Church the hymn became the special medium of religious expression during the early struggle of the Church to attain recognition. Indeed, to maintain its very existence, the hymn served as a kind of battle cry and marching song of faith.

Though contemptuous of other arts, Luther had a fine voice and was a great lover of music, appreciating early the supreme importance of an adequate musical background as an impetus to his newly-launched religious movement. He immediately began the important task of building up a musical service. He set to work amassing, selecting, adapting and creating tunes, poems, hymns and material of all sorts that promised aid. Fortunately, the Germans possessed an enormous heritage of folk and religious songs which had served in the ancient forms of worship.

The rhythmic impulse inherent in secular songs and founded on dance music asserted itself and broke the thousand-year-old tradition of plainsong. Gradually the subjective, emotional spirit of the secular songs and the newly composed music invaded the chorale, and we find that a reformation in Church music had also taken place. *Ein' feste Burg*, one of the mightiest of the German chorales, emerged from this religious upheaval and has, to this day, lost none of its thrilling grandeur. Johann Walther (1496-1570), Ludwig Senfl (?-1555), Georg Rhau (1488-1548), Luke Osiander, Hans Leo Hassler, Johannes Eccard (1553-1611) and Michael Praetorius are some of the more talented German musicians who laboured to improve the German chorale.

In 1600 the organ supplanted the choir in accompanying the unison song of the people. A vast flood of hymns continued to be written, even during and succeeding the Thirty Years War (1618-1648).

In the latter part of the seventeenth and eighteenth centuries, the enervating influence of the Italian operatic aria crept in, displacing the vigorous hymns with pretty, languishing melodies. The influence of the aria,

112

however, was not altogether pernicious. On the contrary, the light-hearted elements it injected into the sturdy, German chorales of the day gave way to the evolution of the glorious works of J.S. Bach: his cantatas, Passions and other choral works. The cantata was the outcome of these external influences and soon gained great favour among the Protestant Churches. It afforded fine means of appealing to the most sophisticated tastes of these centuries, for it combined the Italian aria, the recitative, the instrumental accompaniment, duos, trios, full chorus, and the support of the organ and orchestra. In short, it provided a veritable feast of religious music.

Music of the Anglican Church

With the exception of Purcell and the naturalized Handel, the Church of England cannot boast of such renowned composers as those who so richly adorned the musical services of the Roman Catholic and Lutheran Churches. Nevertheless, the music of the Anglican Church has maintained a uniformity and continuity of excellence which entitles it to high esteem.

In England, musical service has proved as provocative of dispute and dissension as any major doctrine of the two camps of Catholicism and Protestantism. Anglicans and Puritans have contended vigorously over the questions of art and ritual as well as over dogmas in the field of battle and in the arena of forensic dispute. Hence, we must consider two distinct musical systems— the ritual music of the State Church and the psalmody of the dissenters.

We must also consider that in 1534 Henry VIII of England wrenched his country free of papal authority and appointed himself head of the Church of England. This resulted in the suppression of the great English monasteries five years later, practically destroying the principal music schools and crippling the development of English ecclesiastical music. However, Christopher Tye, Thomas Tallis, Robert Whyte and others laboured faithfully to supply music for cathedral services.

At first, Henry VIII was favourably disposed towards the Protestant cause, but the Catholic rebellion in 1536 threw him back into the arms of the established order. Upon the accession of the boy King Edward VI (1547-1553), who had been won over to Protestantism by Archbishop Cranmer, a modified Lutheranism was introduced into the English Church. The people were

113

allowed access to the English Bible. The Book of Common Prayer replaced the Missal and Breviary. The Mass, compulsory celibacy of the clergy, worship of images, and invocation of the saints were abolished.

The first English prayer book in which the English language replaced Latin appeared in 1549. Agitation on the part of the people for a greater simplicity of the musical ritual was stoutly resisted by Queen Elizabeth I, hence the English Church never achieved that degree of informality attained by the Germans. The reformed service restored by Queen Elizabeth has been retained practically unaltered to this day.

One significant figure emerged during the second half of the seventeenth century—the precocious Henry Purcell, a musician and composer of real genius. His church music comprises a great number of anthems and a celebrated work called the *Te Deum and Jubilate in D* for voices, strings, trumpets and organ. His ode, *Hail, Saint Cecilia*, attained great success and is the progenitor of the secular cantata forms developed later by Sir Charles Parry (1848-1918) and Sir Edward Elgar.

The Anglican chant is derived from the ancient Gregorian chant, but its adaptation to the demands of the English language has meant some marked changes. Basically, it is simpler, devoid of the frequent flowery embellishments, is almost entirely syllabic, and is more steady in its management of the rhythm. It is also drier and more monotonous than its more illustrious predecessor.

The anthem, another integral part of the Anglican service, was invented by Purcell and brought to European recognition by Handel. The successor to the Latin motet, it suggests a combination of both this and the German cantata. From the motet, the anthem obtains its massive and impressive choruses, while from the cantata are derived its solos, arias and instrumental accompaniment. The unlimited scope for invention which this form offers has tempted an endless succession of Church composers to produce examples of this form of composition.

Unlike the Roman Catholic ritual, the Anglican service has been little affected by the changing ideals of the music of the salon and the concert stage, and has, with little modification, maintained its earliest sturdy traditions.

Suggested Listening:

Lasso:	*Seven Penitential Psalms*
Palestrina:	madrigals, *Missa Papae Marcelli, Missa Brevis*
Gabrieli:	madrigals
Praetorius:	*In dulci jubilo*
Purcell:	*Te Deum and Jubilate in D* (for voices, strings, trumpet and organ), *Hail, Saint Cecilia*
Mozart:	*Requiem Mass*
Verdi:	*Requiem Mass*

Singing

(12)

a singer's attributes, natural singing, voice training, voice types, the great opera singers

Singing is vocal expression embracing music and words. Beautiful singing requires a healthy body and vocal organs, an alert mind, tonal qualities that are both expressive and pleasing to listen to, a musical ear and good technique. It also demands that the singer, whether performing in his own language or otherwise, fully understands the meaning of the lyrics so that the song or aria has some significance to his audience. In short, and like the conductor, he must interpret his music intelligently so that what he produces becomes an artistic musical experience.

Not all singers, however, are trained. They do not therefore, attain a high level of vocal skill. The "pop" singer, for example, produces his voice quite differently than does the concert or operatic singer. His vocal production, in fact, very often violates all the best principles of artistic singing, especially when he sings with a closed throat, with the voice "locked" in his nose and with distorted diction. Nevertheless, this form of vocal expression is "singing" and the sincerity and feeling it provokes are generally pleasing to performers and listeners alike.

Natural or untrained singing varies from one race to another, because peoples and civilizations have been conditioned by their physical structure, culture, language, climate and general environment. For instance, a Chinese or Japanese folk singer will produce a different sound from, say, a folk singer of the western world. The voices of Indians are unlike the voices of Negroes. The nasal sounds of French, the guttural consonants of German and the open vowels of Italian (which make it an easy language in which to sing), strongly influence the character, vocal styles and quality of sound of singers of those nationalities.

While singing is really nothing more than an extension to speaking, there are some important differences. In singing, the range of the voice is often extensive and the vowel sounds are elongated because it is on these that most tones are produced. Moreover, the singer must conform to musical patterns or design. The speaker, on the other hand, uses a small vocal range and can inflect his voice and determine his rate of utterance at will.

Voice Training

Training the human voice is a highly complex science. Basically, air expelled from the lungs causes the vocal chords to vibrate and these vibrations, in turn, set up other vibrations in the air, filling the oral, nasal and sinus cavities. These cavities act as resonance chambers and give the voice its quality. Full use should be made of them, therefore, and the air should not be forced out through the mouth. The French expression *chanter dans le masque* ("to sing in the face") sums it up perfectly. The singer should feel the notes vibrating in his head, an art which may take time to acquire but which will eventually determine the amount of "ring" in the voice. This so-called "ring" is very important. Not only does it give carrying power, but it is the difference between a bright, interesting and well-focused sound and one which is wide, flat, dead and unable to fill a good-sized concert hall without a microphone.

A singer must also breathe easily and naturally. Countless methods of breathing have been evolved for

117

the acquisition of the proper technique, but the principal condition must always be relaxation of the muscles so that the air can be inhaled smoothly and without difficulty. Surprisingly little air is required for the longest vocal phrase, but this technique cannot be developed without performing breathing exercises on a regular basis. These exercises, in turn, should ensure that the upper part of the chest or the shoulders are not moved and that the column of air that passes up to the throat is controlled by the diaphragm, the muscle dividing the thorax from the abdomen. When breathing in, the diaphragm must be lowered so that the lungs can expand to contain the air flowing in through the nose and mouth. Deep breathing should be carried out calmly and unhurriedly, not too strenuously nor too often. Holding one's breath to stretch the muscles is directly harmful to the vesicles of the lungs.

Intonation is another vital aspect of singing and this depends on tautening the right muscles (and only these) so that the air is afforded clear passage to the nasal and sinus cavities. Nasal exercises demand complete relaxation of the muscles. Jaws, lips, tongue and palate must not be used. The air must flow unhindered through the mouth and nose. Nasal exercises may sound unpleasant, but they are vital if the voice is to carry.

Pure notes are not enough. A singer must also be able to enunciate the words of the song distinctly. Singing is primarily the production of vowel sounds, and since very little alteration in the positioning of the tongue and lips is required to alter a vowel sound, much careful practice is needed in the production of pure vowels. Consonants do not play as important a part as vowels, since they either introduce a note or conclude it. A vowel, on the other hand, accompanies the note throughout its length. In singing, the tongue should lie flat and relaxed in the lower jaw, with the tip against the front teeth; if enunciation necessitates use of the tongue, the tip alone should be used. Some distortion of vowel sounds is inevitable. For instance, it is impossible to sing the sound "ee" on a very high note; and the diphthong has to be produced with almost all the breath and stress on the first part, so that "oi," say, is almost all "aw," followed by a very short "ee."

These hints on singing technique are applicable to voice production in general. Breathing technique, resonance and clear enunciation are the same in ordinary speech. In speech the use of the voice comes naturally.

118

No one thinks about how the sound is being produced or the breathing controlled. Correct singing should be equally easy and natural. The secret lies in muscular relaxation.

In their efforts to develop a powerful voice, many singers are tempted to overdo breathing exercises or to force loud notes. This results in taut muscles, strained and false notes, fatigue, and damage to the throat. Visible signs are tightly-held lips and a quivering chin. A singer should never try to exceed his natural capacity, and one of the prerequisites of a good teacher is the ability to recognize a student's capabilities so that he never sings music too large for his voice or top notes that are not potentially there.

Voice Types

Voice types are determined chiefly by sex and age— namely men, women, boys and girls, youths and children. Further classification, however, is made with special reference to timbre or quality and, to some extent, range. Range, in turn, varies from person to person and depends partly on whether one's voice has been trained. As a rule, the well-tutored adult has a compass of about two octaves, though some of the more exceptional opera singers have been known to produce good quality tones over a span of three octaves.

Men's voices from the higher to the lower are: tenor, baritone and bass.

Corresponding women's voices are: soprano, mezzo-soprano and contralto.

Each of these voices, however, can be divided even further according to their quality and "weight"—aspects which subsequently regulate the repertoire. The tenor voice has more divisions than any other.

Lyric tenor: Light, flexible and high. Suitable for Mozart and Rossini opera.

Spinto tenor: Developed beyond lyric capabilities though retaining some characteristics of the lyric tenor. Not yet dramatic. The most useful tenor voice—suitable for virtually all Puccini and Verdi operas. Some spinto tenors, though, are still able to perform lyric roles successfully.

Dramatic tenor: Heavy, robust, heroic. The least flexible of all tenors. Totally unsuitable for any lyric roles.

119

Usually applied to dramatic roles in some Verdi operas. Wagnerian opera uses dramatic tenors in abundance.

There are two other types of tenor sometimes used in oratorio or for certain light-weight songs of the Middle Ages or early Renaissance. These voices are totally unsuitable for opera, however.

Tenor léger: Extremely light tenor. Much lighter than even the lyric tenor. Usually a high tenor voice, too.

Countertenor: Tenor with the range of a contralto. Sometimes called a "male alto." Often said to be a falsetto voice. It isn't. It is a freak voice produced by head tones.

Marion Anderson was one the the busiest concert contraltos of the century. Since starting her career in the 1920's, she has sung in virtually all the major concert halls throughout North America and Europe. She now lives in retirement.

In the case of basses and baritones, the divisions of voice are not nearly so marked as those of the tenor. The baritone voice is generally heavier than even the dramatic tenor, though lighter than the bass, and comes in two distinctive forms: lyrical and dramatic. Basses are more commonly defined as basso cantate (the more lyric voice) or basso profundo (endowed with extra low notes and usually capable of a larger sound). Basso profundos, by the way, seem to be indigenous to such countries as Russia and Bulgaria and are usually given the dramatic bass roles.

The divisions of women's voices are much the same as the men's. The coloratura soprano is high and extremely flexible. The larger spinto soprano and dramatic soprano voices are less flexible but "rounder." Like baritones and basses, mezzo-sopranos and contraltos are either lyrical or dramatic.

There is another type of voice which now belongs exclusively to history—the castrato, a male soprano who underwent a surgical operation before puberty to prevent his voice from breaking. The practice originated in the East, where harem eunuchs often had high, clear and very powerful voices. Castrati were common in Europe in the sixteenth century, and more than two hundred years passed before the operation was prohibited. The last performance by a castrato in Europe took place in London in 1844. In many countries women were forbidden to appear on the stage, and their parts in opera were taken by young castrati. When adult, the castrato usually had a large body, powerful chest and enormously developed vocal chords, with a high, light

120

voice which far exceeded the female soprano in volume and compass. At the coronation of Napoleon in 1804, the Pope's thirty Sistine castrati, bursting out with their mighty *"Tu es Petrus"* at the moment of crowning, almost drowned the voices of three hundred French choral singers and eighty harpists.

One of the best-known castrati was Farinelli, born in Italy in 1705. The hypochondriac Philip V of Spain had him in his service for ten years. Every evening he had to sing the same four songs to the King, who believed that they had a curative effect on him. Farinelli eventually became the King's personal adviser and died in Italy at the age of seventy-seven.

For a more specific look at singers and their capabilities, I recently went to Hamilton, Ontario, to record a conversation with a former member of the Metropolitan Opera, Mr. Edward Johnson. A spinto tenor, Mr. Johnson sang at the Met from 1947 until 1951. He was following in the footsteps of a distant relative, also named Edward Johnson who, in addition to singing there as a tenor, later became one of the most celebrated Metropolitan Opera general managers.

Author: It's rather difficult, isn't it, to designate some of the best-known singers into the various divisions of voice because in their time they stepped beyond the boundaries, so to speak. Let's talk of some of the important tenors—Bjoerling, Caruso and Gigli.

Johnson: Let's start by talking of Caruso. If you'd heard some of Caruso's first recordings made many, many years ago you'd be surprised how lyric he was. You might not even recognize him. And, of course, the thing that changes your voice is good technique first of all, which you have to have, then maturity—age. The voice is like wine. A good voice will age as wine does. It gets better as it goes on. You get the warmth and depth first of all from good technique. But as you grow older your voice gets darker. It matures.

Author: For instance, Gigli was basically a lyric tenor, wasn't he?

Johnson: Yes, a lyric tenor.

Author: And yet he was able to sing some of the spinto roles.

Johnson: Yes, but you see, in his day, in the early

121

1900's, The Golden Age of Singing, singers spent years perfecting a vocal control that enabled them to do virtually anything they wanted. In other words, singers in those days were called upon to do not only lyric roles, but roles that were fairly dramatic. They could handle these roles, too, because they'd learned how to sing correctly.

Author: I think we must be specific. Caruso was able, was he not, to handle the lyric tenor role in Donizetti's *L'Elisir d'Amore?*

Johnson: Well, sure, he could sing *L'Elisir d'Amore* or Rodolfo in *La Bohème*—the lyric roles. He could also sing Verdi's *Il Trovatore* and *Aida* and so forth, you see.

Author: And Gigli the same, even though he had, perhaps, a smaller voice.

Johnson: Yes, and Gigli the same. But you take even the soprano voices. The sopranos of those days were called upon to do roles which were both large and small.

Author: Let's talk of some of the sopranos of The Golden Age. There was Maria Caniglia . . . .

Johnson: And of course Galli-Curci and Melba, who were coloratura sopranos. But there were some very fine singers of that day—Bruna Castagna, Caniglia—and they were all called upon, even though they were dramatic singers, to do lyric roles that the lyric sopranos of today would never attempt to do.

Author: Let's get back to tenors. Jussi Bjoerling emerges as one of the greatest because he was equipped to do virtually everything. He was, in his day, clearly above everyone else—even Gigli—though some people will not agree with me. He not only sang virtually everything, but sang it well.

Johnson: That's because Bjoerling was in a way comparable to the singers of The Golden Age, even though he came later. Bjoerling had, of course, one of the finest vocal techniques of any singer I've ever heard. With a fine vocal technique you should be able to do anything with your voice, within reason, without hurting it. But Bjoerling was brought up at a time when the emphasis was upon vocal technique and development, which took years. A lot of singers today want to start singing operatic arias after they've studied a year.

Amelita Galli-Curci, the Italian coloratura soprano, was largely self-taught. She nevertheless became one of the finest sopranos of all time—and one of the earliest recording artists. Her favourite role was that of Gilda in Verdi's Rigoletto.

122

Author: And this is usually dangerous for the voice.

Johnson: You've heard the famous story about Gigli, haven't you? He was kept on nothing but vocal exercises by his teacher for five years. When he went to sing an aria, it was like rolling off a log because he had experienced every difficulty that he would ever experience in an aria—by doing these vocal exercises. Arias and songs are really only vocal exercises put to words.

Author: Yes. The same as a sonata for the pianist or violinist.

Johnson: Well, sure. The piano sonata incorporates all the stuff you do when you do your scales.

Author: So, ostensibly, if you do your scales well you'll eventually be able to play anything.

Johnson: Yes.

Jussi Bjoerling was a superb singer of great artistry. Many think that, next to Caruso, he was the finest tenor of all time.

Author: The dramatic tenor voice presents a problem, doesn't it? Most of the dramatic tenors don't have the flexibility and the top notes . . . .

Johnson: No. Most dramatic tenors, because of the fact that their voices are heavier, lack the flexibility in the voice and consequently lack the ability to do the agility work which comes easy to the lyric tenor. The dramatic tenor's voice in the middle of his range almost duplicates the sounds made by a good baritone. There is a very baritonish quality in the middle. But the thing the dramatic tenor lacks normally is the extreme top, although there have been dramatic tenors who could knock off top C's standing on their heads.

Author: Melchior, for example.

Johnson: Yes, Melchior for one. I've heard his top C's. Then, for another, there's Mario del Monaco. But dramatic tenors on the whole are not noted for the top range of their voices.

Author: Yes, but they have power and the dramatic qualities the lyrical singers don't have. Let me suggest something else now. The Golden Age is behind us and singers today are tending to specialize within a confined repertoire. For instance, no tenor in the world today is expected to sing all the things that Caruso and Gigli had to do.

Johnson: But we have one that does—and that's Carlo Bergonzi. He can sing *L'Elisir d'Amore* one night, *Aida* the next, *Il Trovatore* the next and so on.

Author: Yes, and Placido Domingo can, too.

Johnson: But this is where a singer must use his intelligence. He must not try to sing the big roles in *Aida* or *Il Trovatore* like a dramatic tenor. He sings them, instead, with his natural lyric voice. He doesn't try to lead the voice or enlarge it to the detriment of the quality or colour of the voice.

Author: Another thing, too. Today we have a much more intellectual approach to singing, whereas in the days of Caruso and Gigli the Italian language dominated, and singers tended not to be linguists in the way that Bjoerling was and Nicolai Gedda still is today. Caruso's French wasn't very good. Gigli's French was even worse, and his German was abominable. Bjoerling and Gedda, on the other hand, were so well equipped linguistically that they have been able to master operas in three or four languages—and superbly.

Johnson: Yes. In the old days it was sufficient to have a voice and that's all. You could be very stout and go out there and swing your arms like an overweight wrestler and audiences accepted it. The reason for this was that the voice was the main thing in opera. In other words, you didn't have television or movies to zero in on the performer. Today, things are different. We've actually got good-looking opera stars. Take Anna Moffo for instance. She's as beautiful as anyone could be. And there's a much greater emphasis on good linguistics. Patrons of the arts expect it.

Author: We expect a lot of our opera singers today, don't we? We expect them to sing *and* act.

Johnson: Yes. The patrons of the arts expect that when they go to hear a particular singer in an opera, that singer will look the part. Unfortunately that's difficult. Take for example the role of Rodolfo in *La Bohème*. Rodolfo is supposed to be twenty-two or twenty-three. Unfortunately, by the time the tenor is able to sing the role he's in his mid-thirties. Therefore there has to be quite a bit of make-up. People expect to see type-casting, but it's very difficult. They're still seeing Richard Tucker playing Rodolfo and Richard won't see fifty again.

The birth of recording

(13) *the invention of the phonograph, growth of the recording industry, the first recording artists, electrical recording*

Music in the twentieth century has a strong affinity with science. Thanks to science, we not only have electronic musical instruments but radios, phonographs, hi-fi and stereophonic players, and tape recorders, to provide us with replay pleasure.

The task of preserving and reproducing music with fidelity has not been an easy one, but in recent years advances in techniques and instruments have been so dynamic that we now have recordings of unbelievably high quality. Only seconds after a studio performance, artists can hear their renditions and decide whether they are true to their own talents on the one hand, and true to the wishes of the composer on the other. They can also tape and retape over and over again until they are satisfied that what they have produced is good enough for the world to hear.

Today, we take all this for granted, seldom

stopping to think that the musical masters had no such facility of science at their command. They could only write the music for posterity and hope that in future years it would be interpreted and rendered in the true spirit of its creation. They probably never even thought that science would one day play such an important role in the production and preservation of music. By the same token, it is doubtful whether radio and electronics ever entered the minds of the phonograph pioneers. Radio was not invented until 1895. The electron was not discovered until 1896. Yet experiments in recording date back to 1857.

Many inventors, among them a French scientist named Léon Scott, had tried repeatedly but unsuccessfully to reproduce sound. Scott's device, which he called the phonautograph, recorded sound in the form of an undulating line on a cylinder coated with lampblack. The shortcoming that doomed the experiment was the inability to reproduce the recorded material.

History tells us no more of the French scientist, nor of his frustrating effort. But twenty years later, Thomas Edison tackled the idea independently in the United States—and made it work. In so doing, he paved the way for the modern phonograph. Crude as it was, his invention startled the world. He was the first man actually to discover how to reproduce sound, including that of a human voice.

Edison's plan to create a machine that would "talk" came about while he was experimenting with an automatic method of recording telegraph messages. He sketched the apparatus and had his master mechanic, John Kruesi, put the parts together. The machine consisted of a grooved cylinder (around which tinfoil, stiffened with antimony, was wrapped), a diaphragm and needle which rested on the foil, a mouthpiece to speak into, another mouthpiece (or funnel) for outcoming sounds, and a crank with which to turn the cylinder. Edison set the needle at the beginning and recited into the mouthpiece the nursery rhyme "Mary Had a Little Lamb." He then reset the needle at the beginning, resumed his cranking and out of the funnel came a squeaky reproduction of the rhyme. The machine "talked."

Although Edison was already a famous inventor by 1877, he and his associates lacked funds, and one of them decided to try to raise money by lecturing on the inventions. One night in Buffalo, he mentioned that a

126

device for recording sound was under development. The next morning a newspaper headline announced that Edison had invented a "talking machine." A new generic term had been born.

The home entertainment possibilities of Edison's cylinder-type machine were not immediately recognized. The inventor, busy with other projects, gave little or no thought to refinement or to the commercial aspects until several years later when he learned that the rival Volta Laboratories had actually begun filing patents on sound reproduction. Volta, headed by Dr. Alexander Graham Bell, his brother Chichester and Charles Sumner Tainter, brought out the first successful records in wax. Early in the 1880's, they had developed a wax cylinder on which sound grooves could be cut spirally. To play the records they had built what they called the graphophone. Spurred by this rivalry, Edison once more turned his attention to recording. He, too, brought forth a wax cylinder and a machine for reproducing the sound recorded on it. His machine became universally known as the phonograph.

Records of both Edison and Volta were made by the "hill and dale" method—that is the method by which sound vibrations were translated into elevations and depressions in the bottom of the record groove. Both the Edison phonograph and the Volta graphophone employed a special feed-screw mechanism to move the sound box and other connected parts along the cylindrical record. The reproduction quality and the articulation were good, but the volume was so low that listeners had to use ear tubes. These early machines resembled some of today's dictaphones more closely than they did the phonographs that eventually came into service.

Talking machines and records had just reached the public in 1888 when another inventor appeared with a radically different idea. Emile Berliner, a German-born telephone expert of Washington, D.C. (noted for his invention of the microphone), introduced a gramophone which used the world's first flat disc. Berliner called it a "phonautogram." His sytem included a manufacturing technique which provided a master record from which duplicate copies could be made. The first disc had a groove that not only vibrated the phonograph needle to reproduce sound, but piloted the sound box and horn across the record. The record vibrated the needle laterally by means of modulations in the walls of the groove, as

127

opposed to the "hill and dale" method used by his rivals.

Only a few years old, the record industry was suddenly caught in a struggle for supremacy between the flat disc record and the cylindrical record. It had to be one or the other, since the records of one system could not be used on the phonographs of the other. A dramatic succession of advances began when Berliner, aware that his phonograph needed improvements and alterations, took it to the Camden, New Jersey machine shop of Eldridge Johnson, an expert in the mechanical craft. Johnson was fascinated by the talking machine and at once saw its possibilities. He has said: "The Berliner instrument was badly designed. It sounded like a parrot with a sore throat, but it caught my attention and held it fast and hard. I became interested in it as I had never been interested in anything before. The talking machine was a new art with a boundless future waiting only to be developed. The talking machine fever broke out all over me."

Johnson took Berliner's machine and was so successful in improving it that he was given a contract to produce the machines for the newly-formed Berliner Gramophone Co. Johnson also continued his experiments. He developed the first spring-wound motor for talking machines. He made the first successful governor to insure a constant turntable speed. He also improved the sound box. But, above all, he developed a new disc-type record which was superior to any record then on the market. Not only did it provide fine articulation and accurate recording, but it had the added advantage of ample volume and a piloted soundbox—as in the Berliner system. This success, however, came too late to prevent Berliner's company from collapsing. It fell victim to the battle of the cylindrical record versus the flat disc.

For some time afterwards, the outlook also appeared uncertain for Johnson. But out of the wreckage he succeeded in acquiring the Berliner patents to supplement his own, and in 1901 he founded the Victor Talking Machine Company. The name itself served notice on Berliner's enemies of the intentions of the new company. Under Johnson's leadership, the infant phonograph industry was transformed almost overnight into a business of dignity and stature.

Eldridge Johnson felt that only through a supreme musical talent could the phonograph and play-back device be transformed from a "toy" into the greatest medium of home entertainment the world had, until then, known. It needed, he said, box-office names to use it. The Italian tenor Enrico Caruso was willing to lead the parade of artists who were subsequently to prove Johnson's theory and, as early as March 1902, the stage was set for the most significant recording event of all— the event that was to convince the public that the phonograph had changed from an inspired "toy" to a musical instrument of commanding greatness.

Caruso was twenty-eight, and his soaring reputation was in its second year when equipment was set up to make the first recordings in Italy, using the Victor master-disc method. So great was the excitement at the La Scala Opera House in Milan, that the recording staff had arguments and fights over who was to record Caruso. Fortunately, the tiff was settled amicably, and some days later the tenor came to the studio to record ten arias in a single afternoon, with "not one stecca, blemish or huskiness." All ten recordings were processed without a single failure. All ten were issued, and when one of Caruso's favourites, "E lucevan le stelle," an aria from *Tosca*, reached New York and was played for Heinrich Conreid, then General Manager of the Metropolitan Opera, he immediately cabled Caruso an offer of a contract.

Caruso accepted outright payment for his first recording efforts for Victor. Thereafter he expressed a preference for royalties, and his business acumen has since been proven sound. He died in 1921, at forty-eight, from a lung ailment. But to date, record royalties paid to either himself or his estate total more than four million dollars. Furthermore, historians have never been able to decide whether he made the phonograph or the phonograph made him. It is true that he gave respectability to recording, but more than two hundred discs carried his name around the world.

Led by Caruso, other operatic and concert artists ventured into recording. Within a year, the list included such immortals as the French soprano Emma Calvé (1858-1942), one of the finest Carmens of all; the Hungarian violinist Jan Kubelik (1880-1940); the Italian baritone Antonio Scotti (1866-1936); another baritone named Pol Henri Plançon (1854-1914); and John Philip Sousa. They removed the last barriers between performers and the recording studio, and from then on the list grew faster and larger. The first recording in the United States was cut on April 30, 1903. Ada Crossley, a

noted Australian soprano, sang Giordano's song, "Caro Mio Ben." The Irish tenor John McCormack offered his contribution a few months later, and in 1904 Caruso made his first recordings in North America. The violinist Jascha Heifetz, then only sixteen, made his recording debut only a few weeks after his first appearance before the public. And the same year, the Boston Symphony under the German conductor Carl Muck made the first-ever orchestral recording. Not to be outdone, Toscanini, already well known to American concert- and opera-goers and said to have been averse to "mechnical music," made his first phonograph disc.

It was the constant aim of the Victor Company, however, to improve records and instruments in every way possible. Problems were many. More important, leaders of the phonograph industry overlooked radio as an impending competitor. The phonograph was a mechanical instrument. Radio was electronic. In the early days of the phonograph, all recording and reproducing employed acoustical methods. No thought was given to electronics. Sound waves set up by the recording artist caused the recording diaphragm to vibrate and, in turn, actuated the recording stylus. The artists worked

Enrico Caruso, it is generally believed, had the greatest voice the world has known. More than fifty years after his death, people still ask whether the record industry made Caruso or whether he made the record industry. One thing they do agree on, however, is that even on the evidence of poor recordings, his voice was as rich and full at the top of the register as it was at the bottom. It was this flexibility that made it possible for Caruso to master an unusually wide range of operatic roles.

under great handicaps. They spoke, sang or played into a large recording horn which, while suitable for small groups, was totally inadequate for full-sized orchestras. Recording more than twenty musicians presented a serious problem of grouping because it was impossible to bring them all within range of the horn. The usual solution was to pack them on tiered seats. The standard violin could not be used, though. Instead, a special recording violin was required—one with a Stroh horn attached to throw the sound in one direction.

With the musicians packed shoulder to shoulder, it was not uncommon for the violinist to run his bow into the neck or face of the adjacent clarinettist, or for the trombonist to stab the neck of the man in front of him!

In 1925 the confusion ended. One of the most significant developments in the history of the art emerged—electrical recording. The microphone replaced the recording horn. The recording stylus was actuated not by sound waves but by electrical impulses. High and low frequencies never before heard on a record were put onto wax. Next came the orthophonic phonograph, capable of reproducing a wider range of frequencies. Soon, electrical reproduction replaced acoustical reproduction. Steel needles gave way to more durable and more efficient replacements. The record industry was better equipped to flood the world with more and better sound.

The modern recording session

(14) *taping, splicing, cutting the master, processing the discs*

Since the first discs of Caruso's glorious voice were cut, the recording industry has come a long way. Today it involves highly complicated techniques and extremely sophisticated merchandising.

The manufacturing of records means a greal deal of preliminary work, including the negotiation of contracts between the artists and the company, the selection of suitable material, and the clearance of copyright. Thereafter the process moves into the studio. As a beginning, the studio manager ascertains when the artists can all be together at one time, and draws up recording schedules. In the case of a singer and pianist this is simple. When pop musicians are involved, though, it is often very complex. Many artists perform publicly late into the night and are only available to begin recording in the early hours of the morning. It sometimes takes juggling before a time convenient to all can be arrived at.

In one wall of a recording studio there is a large window to an adjoining room or booth from which the proceedings are administered by a producer, and where complex electronic equipment is manipulated by a recording supervisor and any number of engineers. These men spend considerable time setting up their equipment before the artists arrive at the studio. Time is the greatest enemy of recording. It can also be expensive. To record a full-sized symphony orchestra in the United States costs more than $100 a minute, and that is why the producer and his staff must arrive at a session fully prepared, having solved the inevitable problems before they arise.

They may take nothing for granted. What proved successful at the last session may not necessarily be successful at the next. Atmospheric conditions affect the reverberation time of the hall or studio and often dictate microphone placements. At times, these changing conditions make it necessary to move microphones many times during a session, which means that the artists must rehearse their music while the engineers, checking for "balance," work close by. When a large orchestra is involved, this may take many minutes—sometimes more than an hour. But as any recording technician will tell you, it is absolutely imperative. Recordings today have reached a high degree of perfection. This, in turn, means that if the engineers are to reproduce stereophonically an orchestra's magnificent spread of sound, so that it is heard in the living room as it sounded in the studio or concert hall, there is little margin for error.

A recording engineer will also tell you that capturing the full sonic spectrum of an orchestra is usually a much more difficult process than recording a "pop" group. Whereas "pop" music is generally performed with little variation in volume, the orchestra, by necessity, uses a much wider dynamic range. A story, probably apocryphal, about the producer of a recording of Ravel's *Boléro*, makes the point pungently. As many people know, *Boléro* is an unusual example of one long *crescendo*. It starts softly and steadily increases in loudness and orchestral texture until it finally reaches one of the most exciting climaxes in orchestral literature. In order to make the opening sound more impressive, the producer started at a high level. As a result, the opening of his recording sounded better, more full-bodied, more "present" than any other. Progressively, however, it began to sound worse and worse as the engineer was

forced to reduce the level gradually to prevent it from exceeding the limits. Finally, at the end, a midget orchestra was heard somewhere in the distance. It is true that the climax on this recording was probably as loud as any other. But since loudness is relative, the producer had completely wiped out its effect by starting too high and having no place to go. The effect was one long *decrescendo!*

When the producer is satisfied that the microphones are in position and the switches and dials on the apparatus in the booth are properly set for maximum results, a red light appears in the studio. The session is underway.

The first technical step in making a record is to put the performance on magnetic tape. One decided advantage in using this method is that the tape can be edited. If a mistake is made, that portion can be recorded again and spliced into the original in place of the defective portion. Many records you hear actually consist of two or three separate recordings spliced together to make one flawless performance. This eliminates the necessity of having the orchestra do a perfect rendition

The microphones are in place. The balance is set. And Eugene Ormandy is about to begin a recording session with the Philadelphia Orchestra, of which he is musical director.

This is how a recording session appears to the engineer. Note how the interior of the studio is designed to retail full, bright sound, and how the musicians have dressed informally, for the maximum comfort.

at one sitting. The tape recorder is operated by a sound engineer who sits at a desk-type unit called a recording console. From this panel he controls the quality and loudness of the music as it comes from the studio microphones.

The sound, now in the form of electricity, enters the tape recorder, passes through a "recording head," and in so doing produces a varying magnetic field. Simultaneously, a thin plastic tape, travelling at the rate of fifteen inches per second, moves across the head and through the magnetic field. Due to a special iron oxide coating, the tape can retain a magnetic charge. As it speeds by the recording heads, the magnetic field is transferred onto the surface of the tape. Although these magnetic charges will remain on the tape indefinitely, they can, if desired, be easily erased and the tape re-used for other recordings. The finished tape is carefully inspected. It is then run through a magnetic reproducer machine which converts the magnetic energy on the tape back into electrical energy. This electricity, in turn, is used to actuate (vibrate) a cutting needle on a disc recorder.

135

The disc recorder is a machine which makes, or "cuts," records in two sizes—45's or 33-1/3's. In addition to the cutting needle, it consists of a revolving turntable on which is placed a plain (ungrooved) record called a "lacquer." The needle rests on the lacquer, and while the disc rotates it cuts circular grooves into the disc's smooth surface. The final result is the first phonograph record of the original performance. This process may be repeated many times over. The number of lacquer discs produced from the tape, however, depends on the number of records to be made at the manufacturing plant, and the speed with which they are to be produced. Whatever the final number may be, each disc is carefully inspected and tested in the studio, then shipped to a manufacturing plant.

At the manufacturing plant, each lacquer disc is inspected again. Then the plating process begins. The first step is to silver the disc. By mechanical methods similar to those used on astronomical mirrors, a layer of silver is deposited on the lacquer surface, a few millionths of an inch thick. Next, a thin layer of nickel is spread on top of the silver, and finally a thick layer of copper. Then the metal portion is separated from the lacquer, and we have two records—an original lacquer and a new metal "master." This metal master, although a true record of the original performance, cannot be played, since it has ridges instead of grooves.

The master disc, however, is far too valuable to be used in pressing records. Instead, a "mold" is made by coating the master with a thin layer of nickel, followed by a thick layer of copper. The two sections are separated, leaving two metal records—the master and the mold. The master goes to the vaults for safekeeping; the mold is put through still another plating process. In this final plating stage, the mold is given a solid nickel coating. The sections are separated, and again there are two metal discs—a mold and a "stamper." It is the stamper disc that is actually used to make records. The number of stampers made from a mold depends upon the number of finished records to be manufactured and how quickly the job must be done. Throughout the entire plating process the masters, molds and stampers are visually, and, in some cases, microscopically inspected to guarantee they are without defects. Molds, which are metal records and have grooves, are actually "play-tested."

The principal ingredient of the 45 and 33-1/3

long-playing records of today is a vinyl resin, to which is added lubricants, stabilizers and colouring materials. These are carefully measured and placed in a machine called the "banbury mixer," which blends and fuses the ingredients into a soft mass. Temperatures and time have been accurately determined as a result of many laboratory tests. They are also carefully controlled. Steaming hot, the compound is dropped onto two sets of huge rollers which mix it further and flatten it into a thin sheet. The sheet is then cooled. Finally, it is crushed into granular form and stored in large bins for future use. When a record run is to be made, the granulated compound is taken to the pressing department and poured into machines called "preheaters." As the name implies, these machines subject the compound to high temperatures, once more fusing it into a soft plastic mass. An automatic timer controls each machine so that it ejects just enough material to make one record every twenty seconds.

The operation then moves into the pressing department where the finished records are made. Here we find rows of large pressing machines resembling huge waffle irons.

Let's follow the pressing process step-by-step:

- ❖ Two stamper discs (one for each side of the record) are attached to the upper and lower sections of the press.
- ❖ In the middle of each stamper disc an operator places a record label. (These labels are automatically cemented to the record during the pressing operation.)
- ❖ Next, the prepared record compound is taken from the preheater and placed on top of the bottom stamper.
- ❖ The operator touches a lever and from here on the operation is fully automatic. First, the press closes and hydraulic pressure of many tons is applied. At the same time, steam circulates inside the press, softening the compound and forcing the plastic to conform exactly to the shape of the stamper discs. Since the stampers have ridges the plastic record will of course have grooves. After a few seconds, cold water circulates through the press, cooling and hardening the record.
- ❖ The press opens and the operator removes the finished record. However, there remains a rim of

excess material around the record known as "flash." This "flash" is automatically removed by trimming machines in the pressing room.

So highly mechanized is the record manufacturing process today that virtually all important companies throughout the world now have machines which automatically feed themselves with record compound, attach labels, press records, trim edges and stack the finished records into piles.

The musical child

(15) *stimulating the child's interest, selecting the instrument, selecting the teacher, practice sessions, the role of the parent*

Charles Lamb was a brilliant essayist, poet, critic and a literary friend of Coleridge, Hazlitt and Wordsworth. He was also an accounting clerk, a humorist—and a misguided product of the eighteenth century. When he said, "I am incapable of a tune," he was wrong. Modern educators now know that music, as a hobby at any rate, is a skill that virtually anyone can acquire and enjoy.

Any teacher or psychologist will tell you that there is no such thing as a tone-deaf human being. Properly trained, everyone can play a musical instrument with some degree of proficiency. Furthermore, teachers and psychologists know that so far as children are concerned, even the smallest amount of musical training can help form a happier adulthood. Music provides nearly everyone with a wonderful means of self-expression—an emotional outlet that is never lost.

A child's response to music comes early in life. As

a baby, he is quietened by his mother's soothing lullaby. As a toddler, he is happiest clanging a pot cover against a dishpan. In his first grade in school, he thrives on rhythm and song. But converting these musical instincts to musical ability takes guidance and a knowledge of when the child may be ready for lessons. The exact age depends on his individual development. Some children are ready before they go to school, even as early as three, while others may not feel the urge to take music lessons until they are in high school.

It should not be difficult for a parent to tell when a child needs lessons. The youngster may be quick to hum tunes he hears on radio, television or stereo. He may show an early pleasure in musical toys. He may lust to pound the piano keys. If these early signs are not apparent, it is possible the child needs some help. He should be given a chance to hear music—any kind of music. He should be taken to concerts and to hear folk singers and marching bands. He should be allowed to hear music in the home.

Remember that almost without exception, people want to make music. It should not be difficult, therefore, to steer a child towards appreciating it. Music is an important part of education. Reading, writing, arithmetic and music are, perhaps, the richest combination that can be offered to assure a reasonably full and wholesome life. It is never wise to postpone the effort. Life becomes more complicated and busier in a young person's teens, and both the aptitude for learning and the ability to retain information come more easily in early childhood.

The average child, however, does not develop an appreciation for music before he is nine or ten. At about that age he is likely to announce: "Sidney is learning to play the trumpet in the school band," or, "They're giving piano lessons after school. Why can't I take them, too?" This is an obvious cue. A child may not show signs of exceptional talent but may, nevertheless, be as interested in music as in baseball or scouting. An interest such as this should be catered to immediately. It may only last a few years but will lay a foundation now upon which the child may build later.

When it is decided that lessons are in order, the next step is to select the instrument. If the child has a preference and a good reason for it, he should be allowed to decide. If, on the other hand, he has no preference and the parent hasn't either, then the situation should be considered before arriving at a decision. Some instruments are easier to play than others. The saxophone, flute, guitar and trumpet are simpler to master than, say, the violin, the oboe or the harp. A parent should never overwhelm a child with a complicated instrument unless he has real ability and an unusual amount of natural musicality.

It is always wise to choose an instrument that is basic and can provide a proper foundation for any future choice. Almost every musician, regardless of his specialty, has learned to play the piano because it provides excellent groundwork in the structure of music and harmony. Piano music is written in both treble and bass clefs; music for most other instruments is written in either one or the other.

Skill in playing the guitar, piano or even the accordion will inevitably pay off in personal popularity later on; the amateur musician generally finds he has no trouble acquiring invitations to parties. If a young person intends taking part in a group, he might consider such instruments as the trumpet or trombone. If he is sure he can play these well, he will have little trouble joining one of the many bands and orchestras across the country. Most parents, however, choose the piano for their child, and wisely. It is not only basic, but relatively easy to learn, and the upkeep is modest.

Before choosing a teacher, the parent must know the child's needs. That goes without saying, for a bad match can only produce woe. The teacher with the greatest number of Mozarts to his credit may not necessarily be suitable for a child still in the process of early musical development. A teacher who is rich in understanding, on the other hand, would obviously be better qualified to pass on to the child a more profound love for music.

First, then, parents should determine whether child and teacher are likely to be compatible. They should be given the opportunity to talk at some length— to find out what each expects of the other. Some teachers are tough disciplinarians who look primarily for talent and aim for technical perfection. Others are endowed with infinite patience and love of the young and are merely interested in producing children who are musically content. This type of instructor will immediately put the child at ease and make his lessons enjoyable from the start.

Before settling on a teacher parents should talk to

other parents. They should ask whether their child's teacher has a broad musical knowledge and is well trained in his instrument. They should inquire whether he has the ability to infect his pupils with enthusiasm. It would also be in order for the parents to attend some recitals, to judge for themselves the success of various teachers.

Parents should also bear in mind that group lessons are usually less expensive than private lessons—and sometimes just as effective. Many schools offer them at a low cost, and the programmes have been considered eminently successful. With group lessons, of course, a child can progress on a shoestring until it is evident that he needs a more personal form of tuition.

In the first few months of lessons it is debatable whether the practice sessions will be harder on the student or on the parents. But, like growing up, it is something both must endure. Practice periods should always be carefully scheduled so that the young musician acquires a sense of discipline. Early in the morning before school is a good time. Then the child is fresh and able to concentrate. Moreover, he gets the task behind him before other daily assignments seem more demanding.

Parents should always specify the duration of the practice periods, keeping in mind that some children concentrate for longer periods than others. Generally speaking, a daily period of about fifteen or twenty minutes is sufficient for a child under nine. Children between nine and twelve may find that half an hour is enough. Older children will be able to practise for about an hour. Some of the world's great concert artists rehearse their music for as much as six hours on end, and think nothing of it!

More than anything, a parent must be a good listener. There is no point in criticizing or grumbling about sour and wrong notes. Instead, praise should be ladled out generously whenever possible. Furthermore, the young student should be allowed to practise in peace and should be given help only when he asks for it. And when he does ask his parents to listen to a piece of music they should listen. They should also assert their authority when practice schedules are not strictly adhered to.

Finally, parents should never expect to produce an accomplished musician. It may, of course, result. But it

The late Dr. Marius Barbeau, a director of the National Museum
and a distinguished ethnologist and folklorist, sings a Salish
Indian love song to Caroline Price, one of his grandchildren.
He had a special affinity with young people–a very important
quality for those who try to foster in them a love of music.

is unlikely. People who eventually earn a living solely through their music are very few. Parents would be better advised to concentrate on giving their child an introduction to one of life's great pleasures and the unquestionable foundation for the enrichment of his adult life.

SUGGESTED RECORD LIBRARY

The following suggested library of recordings not only embraces the many trends and developments in music's long history but offers at the same time wide and varied listening for all occasions.

Development of the art of orchestration and exceptional examples of instrumental colour and techniques: *Eine kleine Nachtmusik* (Mozart), *Overture to Oberon* (Weber).

Examples of form in musical or historical development of form: *Symphony No. 3* (Beethoven), *Fugue in G Minor* (Bach).

Music for quiet listening: *Air on a G String* (Bach), *Liebestraum* (Liszt).

Programme or descriptive music: *The Sorcerer's Apprentice* (Dukas), *Danse Macabre* (Saint-Saens).

Music suggesting natural phenomena: *La Mer* (Debussy), *The Planets* (Holst).

Characterizations through music: *Till Eulenspiegel's Merry Pranks* (R. Strauss), *Don Juan* (R. Strauss).

Myths, legends and folklore dramatized through music: *The Firebird Suite* (Stravinsky).

Music for correlation with literature, speech and drama: *Romeo and Juliet* (Tchaikovsky), *Peer Gynt Suites* (Grieg).

Holidays and seasons described or observed musically: *The Four Seasons* (Vivaldi), sections of Handel's *Messiah*, an assortment of hymns.

Music for correlation with language arts or study: *Songs* by Fauré (sung in French), *Der Erlkoenig* (Schubert).

Marches: Sousa marches.

Characteristic rhythms: *Boléro* (Ravel), *Take Five* (Brubeck), Waltzes by Johann Strauss.

145

Dance forms: *Minuet in G* (Beethoven), *The Skater's Waltz* (Valteufel), *Swan Lake* (Tchaikovsky).

Nationality in music: *Finlandia* (Sibelius), *Pomp and Circumstance* marches (Elgar).

Choral techniques: "Bridal Chorus" from *Lohengrin* (Wagner), "Grand March" from *Aida* (Verdi), "Unto Us a Child is Born" from *Messiah* (Handel).

Opera: *Rigoletto* (Verdi), *La Bohème* (Puccini), *Don Giovanni* (Mozart).

Religious expression in music: *Mass in B Minor* (Bach), *Jesus, meine Freude* (Bach).

Popular adaptations of the classics: "My Love" (Chopin), "I'm Always Chasing Rainbows" (Chopin).

Great symphonies: Schubert's *Unfinished, Symphony No. 4* (Franck), *Symphony No. 4* (Brahms), *Symphony No. 5* (Dvorak), *Symphony No. 41* (Mozart).

Great concertos: *Concerto No. 5 for piano and orchestra* (Beethoven), *Concerto for violin and orchestra* (Tchaikovsky), *Concerto No. 15 for piano and orchestra* (Mozart), *Concerto No. 2 for clarinet and orchestra* (Weber).

BIBLIOGRAPHY

The following works were helpful in the preparation of this book and will give greater insight into the historical aspect of music.

General Works

Apel, Willi. *Harvard Dictionary of Music.* Cambridge, Mass.: Harvard University Press, 1944.

Bauer, Marion. *Music Through the Ages.* New York: G. P. Putnam's Sons, 1946.

Brinton, Crane. *Ideas and Men.* Englewood Cliffs, N.J.: Prentice-Hall, Inc., 1950.

Cannon, Beekman, Alvin Johnson and William Waite. *The Art of Music.* New York: Thomas Y. Crowell, 1960.

Dorian, Frederick. *The History of Music in Performance.* 2d ed. New York: W. W. Norton, 1966.

Ewen, David. *Great Composers, 1300-1900.* New York: H. W. Wilson Co., 1966.

Fleming, William. *Arts and Ideas.* 3d ed. New York: Holt, Rinehart and Winston, Inc., 1968.

Garvie, Peter, ed. *Music and Western Man.* London: J. M. Dent & Sons, 1958.

Geiringer, Karl. *Musical Instruments.* trans. by Bernard Miall. London: George Allen, 1949.

Grout, Donald Jay. *A History of Western Music.* New York: W. W. Norton, 1960.

Hauser, Arnold. *The Social History of Art.* 2 vols. New York: Alfred Knopf, 1951.

Janson, H. W. *History of Art.* Englewood Cliffs, N.J.: Prentice-Hall, Inc., 1963.

Knobler, Nathan. *The Visual Dialogue.* New York: Holt, Rinehart and Winston, 1966.

147

Lang, Paul Henry. *Music in Western Civilization.* New York: W. W. Norton, 1941.

Lang, Paul Henry and Otto Bettman. *A Pictorial History of Music.* New York: W. W. Norton, 1960.

Leichtentritt, Hugo. *Music, History and Ideas.* Cambridge, Mass.: Harvard University Press, 1958.

Morgenstern, Sam, ed. *Composers on Music.* New York: Pantheon, 1956.

Sachs, Curt. *The History of Musical Instruments.* New York: W. W. Norton, 1940.

Scholl, Sharon and Sylvia White. *Music and the Culture of Man.* New York: Holt, Rinehart and Winston, Inc., 1970.

Taylor, Deems, ed. *Music Lovers' Encyclopedia.* 6th ed. New York: Garden City Books, 1954.

Watson, Jack W. and Corinne. *A Concise Dictionary of Music.* New York: Dodd Mead and Co., 1965.

Music in the Ancient World

Byron, Robert. *The Byzantine Achievement.* New York: Russell and Russell, Inc., 1964.

Diehl, Charles. *Byzantium: Greatness and Decline.* trans. by Naomi Walford. New Jersey: Rutgers University Press, 1957.

Engel, Carl. *The Music of the Most Ancient Nations.* London: The New Temple Press, 1929.

Hadas, Moses. *Imperial Rome.* Great Ages of Man series. New York: Time-Life, Inc., 1965.

Nettl, Bruno. *Music in Primitive Culture.* Cambridge, Mass.: Harvard University Press, 1956.

Reese, Gustave. *Music in the Middle Ages.* New York: W. W. Norton, 1940.

Sachs, Curt. *The Rise of Music in the Ancient World.* New York: W. W. Norton, 1943.

Welesz, Egon. *A History of Byzantine Music and Hymnography.* 2d ed. Oxford: Clarendon Press, 1961.

Werner, Eric. *The Sacred Bridge.* New York: Columbia University Press, 1960.

Middle Ages and Renaissance

Burckhardt, Jacob. *Civilization of the Renaissance in Italy.* New York: Washington Square Press, 1958.

Harmon, Alec and Anthony Milner. *Late Renaissance and Baroque Music.* London: Barrie and Rockliff, 1959.

Meyer, Ernest H. *English Chamber Music.* London: Lawrence and Wishart, 1946.

Pattison, Bruce. *Music and Poetry of the English Renaissance.* London: Methuen, 1948.

Reese, Gustave. *Music in the Middle Ages.* New York: W. W. Norton, 1940.

The Baroque Era

Blitzer, Charles. *Age of Kings.* Great Ages of Man series. New York: Time-Life, Inc., 1967.

Bukofzer, Manfred E. *Music in the Baroque Era.* New York: W. W. Norton, 1947.

Gay, Peter. *Age of Enlightenment.* Great Ages of Man series. New York: Time-Life, Inc., 1966.

Gramont, Sanche de. *The Age of Magnificence* (Memoirs of the Duc de Saint-Simon). New York: Capricorn Books, 1964.

Helm, Ernest Eugene. *Music at the Court of Frederick the Great.* Norman, Oklahoma: University of Oklahoma Press, 1960.

Classicism and Romanticism

Courthion, Pierre. *Romanticism.* trans. by Stuart Gilbert. Cleveland, Ohio: World Publishing Co., 1961.

149

Einstein, Alfred. *Music in the Romantic Era.* New York: W. W. Norton, 1947.

Gilman, Lawrence. *Nature in Music.* 2d ed. New York: Books for Libraries Press, 1966.

Locke, Arthur Ware. *Music and the Romantic Movement in France.* New York: E. P. Dutton, 1920.

Impressionism and the Twentieth Century

Austin, William W. *Music in the Twentieth Century.* New York: W. W. Norton, 1966.

Bauer, Marion. *Twentieth Century Music.* New York: G. P. Putnam's Sons, 1947.

Collaer, Paul. *A History of Modern Music.* trans. by Sally Abeles, New York: World Publishing Co., 1961.

Cornell, Kenneth. *The Post-Symbolist Period.* New Haven, Conn.: Yale University Press, 1958.

Goodrich, Lloyd and John I. H. Bauer. *American Art of Our Century.* New York: Frederick A. Praeger, Inc., 1961.

Hall, James B. and Barry Ulanov. *Modern Culture and the Arts.* New York: McGraw-Hill Book Co., 1967.

Hansen, Peter S. *An Introduction to Twentieth Century Music.* Boston: Allyn and Bacon, Inc., 1961.

Lippard, Lucy R. *Pop Art.* New York: Frederick A. Praeger, Inc., 1966.

Machlis, Joseph. *Introduction to Contemporary Music.* New York: W. W. Norton, 1961.

McMullen, Roy. "Music, Painting, and Sculpture," *The Great Ideas Today.* Chicago: Encyclopedia Britannica, Inc., William Benton, Publisher, 1967.

Read, Herbert. *A Concise History of Modern Painting.* London: Jarrold and Sons, 1959.

Schwartz, Elliot and Barney Childs. *Contemporary*

Composers on Contemporary Music. New York: Holt, Rinehart and Winston, Inc., 1967.

Seroff, Victor I. *Debussy: Musician of France.* New York: G. P. Putnam's Sons, 1956.

Slonimsky, Nicholas. *Music Since 1900.* 3d. rev. ed. New York: Coleman-Ross, 1949.

Symons, Arthur. *The Symbolist Movement in Literature.* New York: E. P. Dutton and Co., Inc. 1958.

Ulanov, Barry. *A History of Jazz in America.* New York: The Viking Press, Inc., 1952.

Musical Instruments

Baines, Anthony, ed. *Musical Instruments Through the Ages.* New York: Walker, 1966.

Harrison, Frank and Joan Rimmer. *European Musical Instruments.* New York: W. W. Norton, 1964.

Marcuse, Sybil. *Musical Instruments: A Comprehensive Dictionary.* New York: Doubleday, 1964.

Sachs, Curt. *History of Musical Instruments.* New York: W. W. Norton, 1940.

Winternitz, Emanuel. *Musical Instruments and Their Symbolism in Western Art.* New York: W. W. Norton, 1967.

Winternitz, Emanuel. *Musical Instruments of the Western World.* New York: McGraw-Hill, 1967.

Jazz

Blesh, Rudi and Harriet Janis. *They All Played Ragtime,* rev. ed. New York: Oak, 1966.

Ellison, Ralph. "Sound and the Mainstream," *Shadow and Act.* New York: Random House, 1964.

Feather, Leonard. *The Encyclopedia of Jazz,* rev. ed. New York: Horizon, 1960.

Hodeir, André. *Jazz: Its Evolution and Essence.* New York: Grove, 1961.

Murray, Albert. *The Omni-Americans.* New York: Outerbridge and Dienstfrey, 1970.

Schuller, Gunther. *Early Jazz: Its Roots and Musical Development.* New York: Oxford University Press, 1968.

Shapiro, Nat and Nat Hentoff, eds. *Hear Me Talkin' to Ya: The Story of Jazz by the Men Who Made It.* New York: Dover, 1966.

Spellman, A. B. *Four Lives in the Bebop Business.* New York: Pantheon, 1966.

Stearns, Marshall. *The Story of Jazz.* New York: Mentor, 1958.

Opera

Ashbrook, William. *The Operas of Puccini.* New York: Oxford University Press, 1968.

Carner, Mosco. *Puccini.* New York: Alfred Knopf, 1959.

Grout, Donald. *A Short History of Opera.* 2nd ed. New York: Columbia University Press, 1965.

Hamm, Charles. *Opera.* Boston: Allyn & Bacon, 1966.

Kerman, Joseph. *Opera as Drama.* New York: Vintage, 1956.

Stevens, Denis, ed. *A History of Song.* New York: W. W. Norton, 1961.

Toye, Francis. *Giuseppe Verdi, His Life and Works.* New York: Vintage, 1959.

Weisstein, Ulrich, ed. *The Essence of Opera.* New York: W. W. Norton, 1969.

INDEX